PAIN AND PROVIDENCE

Pain and Providence

by LADISLAUS BOROS

Translated by EDWARD QUINN

A Crossroad Book
THE SEABURY PRESS • NEW YORK

THE SEABURY PRESS
815 Second Avenue
New York, N.Y. 10017

This is a translation of Erlöstes Dasein:
Theologische Betrachtungen, first published
by Matthias-Grünewald-Verlag, Mainz, 1965

Manufactured in the United States of America.

Copyright © Matthias-Grünewald-Verlag, 1965
English translation Copyright © Search Press Ltd, 1966, 1972

Library of Congress Cataloging in Publication Data

Boros, Ladislaus, 1927-
  Pain and Providence.

  Translation of Erlöstes Dasein: theologische Betrachtungen.
  "A Crossroad book."
  1. Suffering. I. Title.
BT732.7.B613 1975   242'.6'6   74-26563
ISBN 0-8164-2110-2

CONTENTS

INTRODUCTION

THESE six theological meditations are concerned with the most difficult problem facing any thoughtful person: that of human suffering. To attempt to answer this question is to decide whether human life—or, indeed, life at all—has any meaning. Even more: for many, on this answer depends the very existence of God or—if he exists—whether he is a great, merciful and loving lord or a mean, menacing and incalculable tyrant. Human suffering may become the greatest temptation of our existence. How can God look on so much cruelty, injustice and malice, so much oppression of the innocent? Why must his friend suffer just as much as his enemy? Why does he not show his power more clearly? Why must people—our friends and neighbours, for whom we devoutly pray—persist in their fear and despair, without gaining any lasting relief?

So the questions continue. Who thrust me out into this world of suffering, without asking me? Possessed of an immortal spirit, why am I committed to corporality, to transitoriness, to decay? Why is man, the image of God, tormented by infirmity and misery? What is the point of bitterness, desolation and gloom? Why must we pass through death in order to gain immortality, and feel everything torn away from us at the end: our life, our friends, everything too that we have so arduously built up and quarried out? Has such a life still something to unfold? Is there hope of a consummation?

May Christ our Lord grant us power to find his answer to all these tormenting questions, power to win through to his light out of our darkness, to pass over from our despair into his joy. He says of himself: 'I am the first and the last, and the living one; I died, and behold I am alive for evermore, and I have the keys of Death and Hades' (Rev. 1.17–18).[1]

We have used the word 'joy' to express that attitude of mind in which a Christian ought to approach all the problems of his life and therefore also—above all—that of suffering. Joy is the ultimate criterion of Christian existence. If we are depressed not merely superficially, but to the very depths of our existence, then the reason for this cannot be Christian: it is contrary to the spirit of Christ. Our meditations on the dark side of human life—on sickness, suffering and death—ought to bring us joy; otherwise they are not Christian. But joy occurs in Christian existence in so far as a man's life lies utterly open to him who came to us in order 'that his joy might be in us and that our joy might be full' (cf. John 15.11). Christ alone is able to bring light into our darkness. We may look for Christian joy therefore, not by closing our eyes to man's distress, not by turning away our gaze from human darkness, but only by experiencing the outrageous paradox of suffering in its abysmal depths and by opening this abyss to the light of the Saviour.

In our meditations, however, it is important resolutely to hold fast to one thing. After Christ's resurrection the

---

[1] Biblical quotations are from the Revised Standard Version, copyrighted 1946 and 1952. Where the author gave his own rendering I have followed him and these variations are noted.—*Translator.*

fate of the world is already decided: we are on the way towards heaven; no matter how provisional our world may seem to be, the definitive, the final, is already effective there; our questing never comes up against the void; nothing can separate us from the love of Christ. John insists: 'God is greater than our hearts' (1 John 3.20). To all hopes, even to the most extravagant dreams of mankind, Paul gives an answer that surpasses all of them, the Christian answer:

> When all things are subjected to Christ, then the Son himself will also be subjected to him who put all things under him, that God may be everything to everyone (1 Cor. 15.28).

In a world proceeding towards such glory (God will be everything to everyone), there is no reason for despondency or despair. God wants to see joyous souls—renewed, fresh and without care. The Christian must be a herald of joy in our suffering and joyless world.

Life's ultimate questions—and among them are certainly sickness, suffering and death—must be answered in the light of the fundamental insights of our faith: otherwise the answers are not merely too superficial, but simply false. Supreme truths are also the most joyous and the most beneficial. We have no intention here then of 'preaching' to suffering man, but simply of opening up to him the distant horizons of faith until he stands still, gazing in astonishment and forgetting his suffering—if only for a moment.

We know also that for a person who is suffering deeply no merely human consolation is sufficiently consoling. That is why we would like to lead him out of his narrow world into the broad uplands of mystery. We shall speak as plainly as possible about simple and familiar things:

about creation, paradise, heaven; about the selflessness of
those who love, the happiness of those who are silent;
about Christ's friendship for men; about eternal glory
and—above all—constantly about the mystery of Christian joy. These realities have one thing in common: the
longer we meditate on them, the greater, more mysterious and more incomprehensible they become. In all this,
the author had no intention of imposing his own kind of
wisdom on his suffering friends. He has been permitted
repeatedly to experience the mystery of Peter's poverty.
At the gate of the temple a beggar entreated Peter for
alms. 'I have no silver and gold', answered Peter, 'but I
give you what I have; in the name of Jesus Christ of
Nazareth, walk' (Acts 3.6). How fortunate this cripple
was, that Peter possessed nothing.

I

CREATION

At root, suffering is nothing but loneliness, isolation, solitude. Therefore, when we meet a person who is suffering and want to help him in a Christian way, we must try to draw him out of himself. Revelation does this by telling us: 'God created you.' In this statement, which we have so often heard, three mysteries are implied: these we would like to develop a little, one after the other. They are creation, paradise and heaven.

CREATION

We can consider God's creative deed at different levels. The first contains an existential elucidation of our own situation in the world.

Acceptance of our own existence

God speaks through revelation ('God created you') to your existence, as it is experienced in the concrete. You are under my power: I have given you to yourself, just as you are, with all the promise and menace of your life, with your pride and your folly, with what you can achieve and what you are no longer capable of achieving, with your closeness, your weariness, your failure. But also with those things of which you never cease to dream: health, integrity, enrichment, honour, esteem, fullness

of life, human contact, friendship, love and love's full
response; with the possibilities which you perceive in
yourself, with the limitations that close you in. All that
is my grace for you, your createdness bestowed by my
eternal love. I have made known my will through your
very self, through your existential condition, through
your situation at this particular moment, through your
changing states of consciousness: through joy and suffering, through success and failure, through health and sickness, through the little joys of your daily life and through
your deadly satiety making all things colourless. There
is not an event in your life which is indifferent or neutral.
Your existence, just as it is, is worthy of reverence, because it is my grace, the embodiment of my friendship
for you. Venture on your own life: give yourself to me
by the very fact of accepting your life.

If a suffering person promptly says 'Yes' at this point,
he has probably not grasped what is involved and we
have certainly not consoled, but merely confused him.
'Acceptance of one's own existence' from God's hands
involves in fact *the* decision purely and simply. If I
accept my own life too lightly, if I do not feel resistance
rising up out of my innermost being at the thought that
the meaninglessness which I experience as my own is
supposed to be a grace of God (and therefore utterly
meaningful), then I have not experienced God's incom-
prehensibility and in reality do not face God (since a
'conceivable' and 'easily appropriated' God in the last
resort simply cannot be God).

Let us suppose that we love a person in a mature way
and sincerely. Could we really want him to live out our
life and our destiny, to endure all the privations and
poverty of our existence? No! If I love someone whole-

heartedly, I cannot inflict evil upon him to the extent even of thinking that he might be me. And yet that is what God requires of us: to accept ourselves as his grace. If we are to experience our disjointed existence as his grace, we must concentrate on God a whole lifetime long: we must try daily, even hourly, to enter into his inscrutable will which brought us into existence. The acceptance of our createdness becomes perhaps still more difficult when we recall that our existence does not emerge immediately from God, that we do not 'go forth' from his Spirit, like the angels, without intermediary, but that our nature is linked with God as something 'derived': that is, God gives himself to us through the world. This is the second level, the second dimension of our createdness.

Man at the peak of the universe

Man occupies a vertiginous position in the cosmos. He is the peak of the universe, the product of a growth stretching over milliards of years. He reaches down into abysmal depths.

In the first place, he experiences the fact of being planted into a family-community which has shaped him, not only corporeally, but also spiritually. This family-community for its own part enters into what has become historically a cultural unity, into common ways of thought, common preferences, common valuations and agreement about what is to be rejected. This cultural community in its turn is incorporated into the whole historical development of mankind. Thus the individual—mostly, of course, only unconsciously—bears within himself mankind's experience of tens of thousands of years ago. The history of mankind—or, better, that of becoming 'hominid'—must be reckoned at least at a million years. It lies within a continuity of historical development which includes pre-human life. This life goes back at least to two milliard years. Life in turn became possible through the emergence of planets: the planets themselves presuppose the whole development and unfolding of the cosmos from primeval matter, a process which required at least ten milliard years.

Thus man with all his limitations, with his misery and distress, but also with all his promise and hope, stands at the peak of the universe, at the peak of a development stretching down into abysses of time in a way that even today we cannot completely penetrate. The whole cosmos unfolds in the direction of life; life evolves towards consciousness; consciousness in man transforms itself into spirit; spirit is essentially the capacity of being for union with the absolute.

This development presses being as a whole not only 'forwards', but also more and more 'upwards', to God. If a man's individual destiny brings him back to God, he does not thereby merely gain his own perfection, but draws the whole cosmos into the life of God. No one lives, suffers and dies for himself alone. Man's life—and therefore also his suffering and his death—has cosmic significance. Hence we can understand why man's life is a constant 'dreaming forward'. In our inner being we carry the evolutionary pressure of the universe, a pressure that makes itself felt particularly in the form of dreams, desires, restlessness, hope and disquiet.

In every fibre of his existence man feels that he is a being torn apart. What he has already gained gives him no rest. Emerging from the far depths of the past, he is constantly projecting himself into a new future. For man, to be is to be 'in anticipation'. True reality always simply comes upon us. The essence of our being human continues to lie ahead of us. No one can prevent his existence from opening out on to that of another. No one can avoid the secret desire to break out from what has become real, from the restrictions of his state. Man is filled with endless demand. We have ourselves still 'before us'. In all the stirrings of his existence, man perceives that he is driven by a longing, that something which has never existed is trying to break out of his existence, that youth still lies within him awaiting fulfilment.

Incidentally, natural scientists also assure us that the process of human evolution is not yet closed. Man is only at the beginning of his self-unfolding. The probable lifetime of a zoological type of medium size consists on the average of 50 million years. Even if we allow for the tremendous acceleration of evolution which can be perceived everywhere in mankind, we still have some millions of possible future years before us. Man therefore may not consider himself as 'realized' and 'closed', may not give up dreaming; otherwise life will dry up, not only in him, but in the whole universe. In us and through us the world creates itself in its perfected form. The world is a gigantic process of development which—in milliards of years—gradually and fumblingly advancing, ripens towards fulfilment. A process in which man has to lead forward the line of life's total striving by his deliberate decision.

The whole universe—man included—is a unity of becoming. God creates the world by giving it the resources, in a slowly ascending development, to take on the shape of man; and through man, through his deliberate

2

decision for God, to enter into eternal glory. The universe as a unity of development therefore becomes more and more a common striving, comes more and more to a head, thrusts forward indeed to an absolute peak—to heaven. This contraction of the whole process of evolution in man engenders in him a tremendous pressure of ideas, desires, dreams and hopes. It is constantly fermenting and simmering within us. Giving meaning to all these hopes and dreams is a perfected reality: the cosmos already entered into eternal glory, heaven. When we try to give more profound meaning to these leading ideas, we discover a third dimension of the reality of creation.

Linked with the eternal procession of the Trinity

As we press forward in this way, we perceive God himself, his creative efficacy at work in us. When he considers his position in the universe as a whole, man finds that his life has inestimable worth. What is there of inestimable worth in us? Revelation tells us that we bear within ourselves the life of God. When we say—as we commonly do—that God creates us out of nothing, we are bringing out merely the negative element in the definition of God's creative activity. The true and positive reality of creation is this: God makes us out of nothing other than himself, according to no other pattern, no other law, under no other influence.

Everything created lives as thought and image of God, the expression of his innermost will. If we want to fathom the deepest mystery of our createdness, we must do so by reflecting on the mystery of all mysteries, the eternal procession of the Godhead. God is triune, revelation tells us: he is a 'procession'. That procession by which in God there are three who utter 'I' and three also who say 'thou', although it is one single essence which pronounces this. A procession in which God confronts himself personally and so loves this one confronting him that this love of his itself is someone, the Holy Spirit. God is eternally originating: eternally engendering and bestowing himself as Father; eternally going forth, lovingly responding, as Son; eternally returning, young love of giving and receiving, as Spirit.

Through our createdness we are united with this eternal procession of the Trinity. Everything created is linked in a mysterious union with the second divine person, with the Logos, with the Son. The Logos is the perfect self-expression, the image of the Father, an image that confronts the Father and yet is himself; an image in which God knows himself perfectly. In this perfect image of God—which is, of course, his self-knowledge 'become' a person—lies the reason for the very possibility of creation, of a finite likeness of the nature of God. Everything created is by the fact of bearing, and in so far as it bears, the characteristics of the second divine person.

This, however, does not mean that God created the world simply at the beginning. The whole world is permanently rooted in God's creative activity. Our theology does indeed distinguish between 'creation', 'conservation in being', and 'concurrence'. Nevertheless, these three 'activities' of God, placing a finite thing in existence, unceasingly tearing it away from the menace of nothingness and endowing it with the power of causality, considered from God's side, are not three different acts, but only three aspects of the one creative deed. And this means that the creative act is not merely the past, but also the sacred present moment. From moment to moment the world emerges from God's eternal hands in the freshness of creation. 'At the beginning, God created heaven and earth', is true of this very moment in which we are living. Thus every kind of creature, matter or spirit, is in an ontological immediacy to God.

What distinguishes spirit particularly among all creatures is this: spiritual being has to realize its immediacy to God freely and consciously; not only must God be close to it, but it must itself find a way to immediacy to God. This capacity in us for a deliberately realized immediacy to God we call the spiritual soul. Through it man is able to enter into the depths of the Godhead, to the heart of the universe. This is the splendid dignity of being man: through knowledge and love of the second divine person, to make the world—which 'flows out' from God through the second divine person—flow back into the Godhead. That is: to gather the world up into himself and carry it on to its final consummation.

These perspectives of our createdness really disperse all commonplace ideas. They give to human existence the radiance of a sacred beauty. At the same time, these truths rise menacingly before us. How then is it possible not to live my nature as the crown of the universe and the thought of God? My whole existence ought to be other than it is. I ought really to be able to love God wholeheartedly and sincerely, to be present in the world as a mighty spirit and in deepest harmony with him who created me. 'Yes,' revelation tells us, 'that is what man ought to be.' But he is not that. Why?

If we find an answer to this 'why', we shall have grasped the deepest reason for human suffering. But first let us recall two surprising statements of revelation: there was a time when man's nature fully realized its immediacy to God; and there will be a time when human immediacy to God will develop into a state of being. In regard to this, God himself gives us the staggering information: the situation in which you live, as suffering man, is an interim period of misfortune in a world created for happiness. It was not always so and it will not always so remain. Originally, mankind lived in the state of integrity, of knowledge of essentials, of impassibility and of immortality: in paradise. It will again one day live integrally, knowing, impassible and immortal: in heaven. These two statements of revelation we now want to grasp as living truth: that is, not only with the understanding, but with our whole heart.

PARADISE

'Another' world

To describe the primal state of mankind the Bible uses the picture of a peaceful, enclosed garden. It is a garden full of blooming and fruitful trees, which provide refreshing shade; cool waters flow through it. Man lives in complete harmony with nature, calls the animals by name, even 'sees' God himself in the cool of the day 'walking' in the garden. A world stands before us, filled with peace and beauty. The garden is a metaphor and really means the whole world. The sense is then: at the beginning, man lived in another world. In what sense was this world 'other'? It was certainly a very hard and menacing world, for primitive man had not yet been able to master it. Nevertheless, this man lived in another sphere of existence, in another world. Here we must first of all raise the question: what is really meant by 'world'?

'World' arises out of two constituents, from the 'worldliness' of the world and from consciousness: that

is, from the things, men and events which surround us
and from our mental attitude, from our state of awareness. The 'world', then, is not a factor already at our disposal. It 'happens', because of objective facts and because
of our subjective attitude to these.

Today we still experience something of this kind in
love and in friendship. A person who loves experiences
the world differently: in relation to the beloved 'thou'.
He discovers in the world other depths and new meanings. Something analogous occurred in the state that we
call 'paradise': only more powerful, seizing man's whole
structure of experience and thus transforming his world
from within. We find the central element of paradise
described in a casual, pleasant observation, apparently
secondary to the main biblical account: 'They heard the
sound of the Lord God walking in the garden in the
cool of the day' (Genesis 3.8). This means that between
the Creator and his creature there still prevailed an experienced 'immediacy'. For this man God was the 'sphere
of life that he really lived'; everywhere, he felt that he
was close to God.

Romano Guardini says:

> Let us imagine that man—with whom we are concerned—
> is what he came to be from the hand of God: full of life,
> free, joyous and whole. In his heart there stirs no lie, no
> cupidity, no revolt and no violence. Everything in him is
> open to God, in pure harmony with him who created the
> world. He is bathed in his light, sure of his love, obedient
> to his direction. If it is this man who confronts things,
> what sort of a world then emerges from his seeing, feeling,
> action? It is paradise. 'Paradise' is the world as it constantly
> grows, breathes, develops, around that man who is the
> image of God and tries to realize this image more and more
> perfectly. The one who loves God, obeys him and con-
> stantly calls back the world into holy unity.

This person knew about God: he knew indeed as a result of constant, intimate conversation with him. In his spirit was God with all the might of his reality. We may say then that paradise was the same world in which we also live, and in fact even more dangerous and menacing. Nevertheless, it was another world because man experienced it differently, as immediately from God. Or, if you wish, it was not another world but a world experienced otherwise.

Theologians describe man's state in paradise in this way: he was 'whole' (*donum integritatis*), 'knowing' (*donum scientiae*), incapable of suffering (*donum impassibilitatis*) and 'undying' (*donum immortalitatis*). These 'preternatural gifts' represent an almost complete existential systematization of the true human reality. The whole lot can be traced back to that central factor which we mentioned above: the experience of immediacy to God.

Nature acquired in experience

Man in paradise was inwardly whole: that is, he was not torn apart, divided between desire and realization. He was able to gain his nature (his longings, his dreams, his expectations) personally, in experience. Of course he must also have known what it was to go on yearning for something. Man is essentially a being in process of becoming (*substantia potentialis*). What he is, always lies ahead of him. He must 'dream himself into' his true nature. In order to be, he must take the future by storm. Tension is his very nature: he is stretched out towards something still greater. In him there always yawns an abyss between being and yearning, between realization and dream. Even in the paradisial state, man's nature

was constantly 'ahead' of him. But, through his direct experience of God, he perceived the fulfilment of all his
longings in his immediate environment. He knew from
intimate experience that all desires and dreams have their
fulfilment, that no tracks of men end in trackless waste.
In this way man was 'whole' in paradise: filled with
longings, but perceiving quite close the fulfilment of
these longings.

Another view of the world

We may presume that paradise was not a state of
'quantitatively' developed and articulated knowledge.
The first man certainly lived still in a twilight state of
consciousness. Systematic knowledge of mankind, given
expression and dominating the world, is the fruit of a
very long tradition, a collection—so to speak—of individual experience and insights. It is highly probable
that man at the beginning was 'quantitatively' lacking
in knowledge to such an extent that he would have gone
mad in our world, so largely under the control of the
intellect. Nevertheless, 'qualitatively', he knew more
than we do. The little—the very little—that he did know,
he had grasped in its ultimate reason, in the source of all
being. He experienced the world as the transparency, the
translucency of God. He was in a world radiant with
God. His experience of the immediacy of God effected
in him another view of the world: he saw right through
things to their ultimate reason; he saw God in all things.

Not overwhelmed by suffering

The state of paradisial impassibility again must not be
thought of as an enchanted world, without sickness,
without pain, without bodily afflictions. The more finely

and highly developed a creature is, the more sensitive it
becomes to pain. This holds particularly for man. From
all that we know of man, from the purely corporeal
standpoint, he is inferior to all animals. He is not adapted
to his world. And there lies his unprecedented chance in
the world. He does not adapt himself to the world; he
changes the world, adapts it to himself. In order to do
this, he must know at what points the world can become
a threat to him. He must have signals to make him aware
of the menace, if he wants to survive in this world. These
signals are the feelings of pain. A man who felt no pain
would not be able to continue to exist in the world at all;
without pain, he simply would not be a match for his
world. But if a person continuously experiences his immediacy to God, if he is wholly wrapped up in the other,
in God, then pain cannot 'overtake' him; it cannot seize
hold of his nature, that is, it cannot become suffering in
the proper sense of the word. Even today, love provides
us with an example of this. A lover may feel pains, be
tormented in soul and menaced in body; if he loves and
by the very fact that he loves—that is, if he is drawn with
his whole being into the beloved 'thou', he bears within
himself a happiness that cannot be touched by any suffering. Impassibility in paradise was probably no more than
the knowledge that man is secure in the love of God.
This direct awareness can coexist with bodily pain,
earthly affliction and temporal loss.

This, too, is similar to what the saints experienced.
Francis of Assisi in the midst of appalling misery had to
pick up two pieces of wood and pretend to play the violin,
he had to sing and dance. Sheer joy made Francis Xavier
behave like a child at play, throwing an apple into the air
and catching it again, while he was wandering, stripped

of all he possessed, overwhelmed by failure, hungry, through the icy, wintry countryside of Japan.

Passing over without fear to God

In the state of original justice man was immortal, but not in the sense that he would have been able to continue forever living his biological-finite life. Biological life has to unfold itself. But in so far as this unfolding and development take place, it is refined to such a degree that further life becomes impossible: it becomes brittle. With fertilization existence first of all enters into a phase of steep ascent, then passes through the stages of growth and maturing. During this time there is a progressive differentiation of the potentialities within that existence. There follow the phases of weakening and decline; finally, the catastrophic stage of dying. At the beginning there occurs in the organism a kind of explosive unfurling of vital forces. They are generously set to work, even thoughtlessly squandered. Physiologically, man lives with such a drive at the beginning that he seems to be falling over himself. But slowly the vital energies dwindle and he begins to draw on his reserves. The impetuosity of youth slows down; vital forces flow more and more thinly. The living being becomes utterly exhausted. What at the beginning was an elastic bodily structure becomes brittle and rigid: it loses its adaptability and in the end it breaks like a piece of dry wood.

In the very process of expansion, life prepares for its breakdown, proceeds towards death. But in the state of experienced immediacy to God, this death would not have been a 'dissolution of the body' (*mori in corpore, exire a corpore,* according to Canon 1 of the Council of Carthage). By God's power, man would have 'engen-

dered' himself immediately into the state of consummation, into that of the resurrection into heaven. He would
not have experienced death in the proper sense: dying,
the pains and agony certainly; but not death, not the dis-
solving of his own being. The immediacy to God, in
which he had lived, would have created in him an immediacy of resurrection, of heaven.

Let us try to express what we mean from another angle.
For us men, distant as we are from God, the encounter
with him is always painful and means an upheaval of
our whole existence. Scripture describes the encounter
with God as taking place in this way: man craves for
God with his whole being; but when he catches sight of
God, he has to cover his eyes, he falls down like one dead
(see the 'epiphanies' of God to Moses, Elijah, Isaiah,
Daniel, Ezekiel, the vision of the three apostles on the
mountain of the Transfiguration, and also the opening
vision of the Book of Revelation). For us, God is 'deadly'
strange: when we die, we are in fact in deadly fear of
him. But if a person had spent his life in the experience
of friendship with God, he would have been calm, would
have passed over to his friend unafraid and undismayed;
he would not have experienced death—not real death—
although, purely on the surface, his dying would have
been no different from ours.

That is how human life was originally conceived and
created by God. Not closed up within itself, but wholly
'drawn out' towards the Holy, the God of experience.
This man might well have been ever so coarse, imperfect,
rough, ignorant, imperilled and mortal; he was nevertheless finished. Paradise—whether it lasted for a long time
or only for a moment, is of no importance—was a state
of being, calmly, knowingly, fearlessly and richly lived,

in the midst of a turbulent, gloomy, imperilled world, doomed to death. This life no longer exists. Somewhere paradise was destroyed. We were exposed to inward divisions, to ignorance, to suffering and to death.

Who caused this situation? Certainly not God. He never breaks off a friendship. In some fashion—we cannot say, where and how and why—man told him to his face: I will no longer live with you. That 'No' destroyed the loveliest, truest, most vital reality in this man: his immediate relationship to God. He could no longer directly experience God. Thence all his longings became vain; thence he had abandoned himself to existential ignorance; thence pain rose within him, overflowed his whole being and turned into suffering; thence out of dying came death.

One thing, however, we must recall with astonishment. God did not let it rest there: he did not abandon man. God himself—'in his despair', we would really have to say, if the expression were not inappropriate—took suffering on himself: he descended into death. He could no longer hold back the suffering breaking in upon us. Therefore he entered into suffering with man. As man drew away from God, God came closer to him, bestowed his presence on him again and again, until he completely overtook man, becoming himself wholly man, taking to himself our fragile nature, our peril of body and soul, our suffering and our death. Since man no longer wanted to be with God, God became man. Why he did that, we do not know. Love has no reasons. Love gives itself without reason and that is just what makes it love. And God is love, revelation tells us. He not only loves, but his very being consists of love. He loves and does nothing else but love. To love and to be, in him, are one. He would no longer be—an absurd supposition—if he were no longer to love.

By becoming man in Christ, God accomplished a second act of creation. He made heaven possible for us again. Creation, therefore, is not yet completed. It still goes on. It comes to an end when man yields himself afresh to the consciously experienced immediacy of God, when he enters heaven.

In order to be able to understand our life of suffering, we must know—and indeed not only know, but inwardly experience and credibly show to our friends—the fact that human life was designed for heaven. The world really begins only when man enters heaven. The world is built for heaven. The end is the beginning. Our life is a growth towards heaven. Heaven is the world 'created' for ever.

Thus we come to the third point of our meditation. God tells us in his revelation: the state of sickness, suffering and death will not last eternally; it is a transitory, provisional condition.

HEAVEN

What really is 'heaven'? We do not know exactly. The abbreviated form of expression used in the Bible for the final consummation is 'the new heaven and the new earth' (cf. Rev. 21.1). That is how the Hebrew language described the universe, for which it had no proper word. John describes this new world in his 'Revelation'. He speaks of seas of glass, of streets of crystal gold, of gates formed out of a single pearl, of walls constructed with radiant jewels (cf. 21.18–21). In this description emphasis

is laid on the prodigious, on the humanly unattainable.
Paul also insists that heaven is wholly different: 'What
no eye has seen, nor ear heard, nor the heart of man conceived, what God has prepared for those who love him'
(1 Cor. 2.9).

Nevertheless, heaven is already close to us. With
Christ's resurrection and ascension, heaven has already
dawned. The forces of the future world have already
taken possession of us. Christianity regards the resurrection of Christ, not only as his personal destiny, but simultaneously as the first sign that in our world, in the true
and decisive depths of reality, everything has already become different. The Easter event is not an isolated pheno-
menon of redemptive history, existing on its own account,
but the sacred destiny of the whole world. In his resurrection Christ uttered over the whole universe his creative
word: It has begun. 'Behold, I make all things new'
(Rev. 21.5).

'Distant' and yet already 'close'

Heaven is still 'far away' from us. But at the same
time it is close, radically akin to us. In this tension the
Christian lives. In a sense he is already in heaven, but
in a heaven still awaiting him. The disciples on the way
to Emmaus had a similar experience of the reality of the
risen Lord. Christ joined the two disciples who had left
their brethren gathered in the upper room. He went a
long way with them, spoke with them. But they did not
recognize him. After his resurrection, the Lord always
appeared in this way: always unobtrusively, as one
hungry, as a gardener, as a wanderer, as a man on the

shore. This is the way in which heaven also is close to us. It appears in unobtrusive forms, in reflections.

Life lived intensively

The final consummation, heaven, is God's definitive closeness which can no longer be destroyed: participation in God. But his infinite fullness cannot wholly be taken in or exhausted by any creature. Our being can never completely coincide with God's. Every fulfilment is simultaneously a new beginning, the commencement of a still greater fulfilment. Heaven must be understood essentially as dynamism without limit. Fulfilment itself will so 'expand' our soul that in the very next moment it can be filled still more with the being of God.

We are eternal seekers after God. God always remains greater than our finite being. The God who is finally 'discovered' is not God. We seek God in order to find him, in our earthly life. We seek God after we have found him, in eternal bliss. So that we may seek him in order to find him, he is hidden. So that we may seek him after we have found him, he is infinite. Our eternity will be an everlasting advance towards God. Everything static becomes in heaven absolute dynamism, projecting into infinities. Consummation is eternal transformation, the state of unbounded, unbroken vitality.

Transformation of our worldliness into 'heaven'

It is in the light of all this that sickness, suffering and death must be considered. These are the true perspectives of human life. We are not abandoned for ever to suffering. Our inward derangement—even corrosion—does not last eternally. We are on the way to heaven.

What befalls us here by way of suffering and distress is provisional and therefore also—in its deepest and ultimate meaning—secondary. By deliberately laying himself open to heaven with Christian resolution, man works at the creation of the world.

Here, finally, another aspect of 'becoming heaven' should also be mentioned: heaven will arise for the others—for those whom we love—in us and through us. Our solitary wrestling with God here on earth has eternal import. We create the final world: we become heaven for all those whom we love. That dimension of heaven which God sets up in us and through us would never emerge, if we did not now lay ourselves open to God's power. In a world doomed to suffering, our own personal quest for God is a work to be shared by those whom we love—indeed, by all mankind and even further by the whole universe. It is—so to speak—a forward thrust to the last outposts of the world, to the point at which the transformation of our worldliness into heaven takes place. On the quest for God, for my own part, I am the most advanced and highest peak of cosmic development. Searching for God in this way, I am making the greatest possible gift to those whom I love. I am transforming myself into heaven for those I love. The quest for God is the most tender act of my love to a human 'thou'. I make his heaven, his eternal consummation, richer, brighter, mightier.

At the end of all seeking, wandering and suffering, there is the promise of eternal happiness. It will be a state such as that of which John in his 'Revelation' speaks: the real, the uniquely real, God will no longer be inaccessible and hidden. Then real life begins. In God's eternal-single deed, beginning and consummation in one, there was 'wedged'—so to speak—an interval for creation's self-development: an interval in which the world by God's power struggles through milliards of years of becoming to consciousness and freedom, in order finally—through man's conscious and free decision for God—to transform itself into a universe wholly radiant with God, into a divine sphere, into heaven. Summed up in a single sentence, this is the 'history' of creation. God creates the world through us and in us.

II

CORPORALITY

THE meditation on creation made clear how closely man's existence is bound up with that of the universe. The point at which we are most deeply rooted in the universe is the body. In the human body, the world rises up into the spiritual sphere. Our body is the place chosen for this transformation, for the cosmic leap into what is qualitatively 'other'. This is our predestination; it is, at the same time, our peril. Here lie the reasons for man's dignity and man's suffering. Anyone who wants to understand the essential structures of human suffering must first reflect on the human body.

MAN AS BODY-SOUL UNITY

As a basis for our meditation we would like first to outline the profound, but often misunderstood teaching of St Thomas Aquinas on the relation of the spiritual soul to the body.

The soul as 'form' of the body

According to Aquinas, man is a single being in which matter and spirit are principles substantially united in one wholeness. In this theory, man is not made up—so to speak—of two 'things'. The whole body and its whole activity are simultaneously a work and an activity of the soul. Man's spiritual soul is the form of the body down to its last fibres and deepest stirrings. On the other hand, the body enters into the spiritual realm in such a way that it belongs to the inward perfection of the soul. So much are body and soul one in us that in this oneness their duality completely fades out. From the two emerges a third that is not either of them. The one substance, 'man', is not a union of two substances, but a single, complex substance—which, however, owes its substantiality to one only of its constitutive principles, namely, the soul.

'Deployment' of the soul

The body, then, is the soul's 'deployment'. In its entire range, our body is a self-expression of the spirit-soul, precisely because the soul is in the body immediately as in that which gives it scope. In St Thomas Aquinas this conception is based on the doctrine of 'unity of substance'. Corporality is not 'attached' to the soul by a superficial-accidental relationship: rather is it established in reality by an essential act of the soul; by an act, therefore, that is not distinct from the soul's essence. The relation to corporality belongs to the essential constitution of the spirit-soul. Without this relation the soul is not a soul at all. The body then is comprised in the soul from the very beginning. This essential relationship, however, does not arise between two beings, as it were perfected in their essential constitution, but is present in them prior to all other types of relation and makes them what they are: body and soul.

The bond between body and soul is a 'transcendental relation', that is, a basic relation present at all levels, in every attribute and all other relationships of soul and body. Everything that comes to the surface in corporality is a deployment of the soul, deployment of what is originally and implicitly (*originaliter et quodammodo implicite*) already contained in the spirit-soul. By an inner necessity (by that necessity which alone makes it soul), the soul 'releases' corporality out of itself. And on the other hand, by an inner necessity (which makes it body), the body 'demands' the soul.

Pivot of cosmic development

This teaching—perhaps formulated a little too abstractly—will enable us to understand what man really is. We cannot come into contact with a human body without in some way touching the soul, and vice versa. Already the body is always soul and the soul already is always body. Here is expressed a whole—we might say, 'revolutionary'—theory of human love, of medicine, of friendship, and of human relationships altogether. It is only through this relationship that in man the universe can really pass over into the spiritual realm, can really become spirit.

As we have already explained, the world has been from the beginning (and still is) a unity in process of transformation. The trend of the universe can be seen to favour the more complicated, more inward, more unified. With the higher development of life this tendency became ever clearer and more pronounced, until in man finally the great leap forward took place: life became refined and receptive to such a degree that it was able also to 'accommodate' the spirit. When we try to understand it retrospectively, we cannot avoid the impression that the whole development of the universe is dominated by an urge towards 'spiritualization'. Aquinas's teaching on the body-soul unity provides us with the fundamental principles behind our assertion that in man matter really entered into an ontological unity with spirit. It is only through this teaching that we can formulate the real meaning and explanation of evolution: in man all the material energies of the universe are concentrated and break through into the realm of the spirit. Thus the human body is the pivot of cosmic development.

MAN AS UNITY OF BODY, SOUL AND GRACE

Thomistic teaching on the body-soul unity gives us important and essential information about our position in the universe. Nevertheless, it is not the deepest possible level of thought. Augustine with his keen mind comes closer to this in a thought-provoking suggestion thrown out as an aside—'with the left hand', so to speak. This is the doctrine of the 'body-soul-grace' unity; the designation is not a familiar one, but coined by us as an abbreviated formula. Augustine describes human wholeness of life in a very striking sentence: 'the life of the body is the soul, but the life of the soul is God'. This statement takes us deeper into the human reality than the teaching of Aquinas. Above all, it sheds light on how we—who are, so to speak, the crown of the universe— can be stricken with suffering and sickness, how therefore our vital unity is broken.

'The life of the body is the soul.' The first part of the sentence does not take us beyond Aquinas. It simply says the same thing in a different way. The essence of the human body consists in the fact that its vitality does not originate from the body itself, but flows out from the soul as from a source of being. It is the soul alone that

makes the body really alive. The spirit therefore is not
the adversary of the body, but the very opposite.

'But the life of the soul is God.' This second part of
the sentence revolutionizes our commonplace views of
man's nature. It is from God alone that the human soul
becomes alive. This vitality is called grace. Only that soul
which consciously and lovingly realizes its immediacy
to God really lives and is able to pass on life to the body.
If now we join together again these two parts of the sentence, we have an astounding interpretation of the whole
world-reality, an interpretation at once anthropocentric
and theocentric.

'The life of the body is the soul, but the life of the soul
is God.' A man endowed by God with grace represents
a special unity: the whole man lives—so to speak—from
above 'downwards' and becomes in all the structures of
his being God's revelation, the herald of the invisible.

The Fall interrupts the development of the world-whole

Today this wholeness of life no longer exists. Sin has
shattered it. The life-giving flow of grace was interrupted.
Thus the soul forfeited its power to be wholly master of
the body, to find in this complete self-expression and
absolute self-realization. The radiance, the true reality,
the vitality of man has thus been lost: that primal reality
which, out of the whole universe, became concentrated
in man and through him—through man's deliberate
choice—sought to struggle upwards to God.

From this it is clear that the Fall was an indescribable
catastrophe, and indeed not only for mankind, but also
for the whole cosmos. Through it the drive of the universe towards God was arrested. According to God's
original plan and by his power, through the human spirit

with which (in man's body) it is essentially united, the world was to have entered into an eternity of being with God. But sin erected a dam against this cosmic flow. Thus all the energy of the developing universe was stopped up in human existence and there turned into a destructive power. This congestion of energies created in man a whirlpool of tensions, agitation, breakers, which in our consciousness took the form of restlessness, disquiet, cruelty, violence, and in human history of combat, war, destruction and hate.

Christian witness lays open the world-whole to God

God wanted to set the cosmic development in motion again. He could not look on while his creation was perishing. Therefore he made a radical intervention into world-reality and in Christ became a man, entered into death and thus penetrated the breakwater of the world: through this opening cosmic development can now flow onwards. Already in his resurrection and ascension, by rendering possible for us a new immediacy to God, Christ led the world to its eternal consummation. Man as ontologically realized unity of body, soul and grace can therefore become whole again only by passing along the same way as that which Christ trod for us: through death and through that which Christ made of death, through the resurrection and ascension.

Although the full realization of the 'body-soul-grace unity' will be possible for us only in death, nevertheless the Christian's mission in life consists in witnessing to this state even now, in growing constantly closer to God, patiently ripening in soul and body. In a daily renewed effort, the Christian must make his whole being—therefore his spirit and through this his body—'radiant with

God'. This effort is called Christian witness. It is therefore not merely a kind of pious practice, but the restoration of the state of the world as planned by God. By this testimony, the Christian lays human nature again open to God: that is, he begins to live as truly man, as unity of body, soul and grace. In the Christian struggle of living on the friendship of Christ—that is, on grace—in a world of darkness and divine impenetrability, the universe is again 'set in motion'. The body becomes alive again, joy again attainable, the world spiritually radiant, the universe again open to God.

From this standpoint wholly new perspectives are revealed to us. The human body as we know it is merely a pale reflection of what man's body really ought to be. The true character of human corporality becomes visible only in the risen Christ. In him, as he attains his resurrection, we reach true human corporality. So we come to the three following points of our meditation: the inappropriateness of our corporality; the consummation of the body in the risen Christ; the risen human body.

THE INAPPROPRIATENESS OF OUR CORPORALITY

Our earthly 'disruption' is due to our corporality. This is not a 'platonizing' statement. We mean to say that we are inwardly 'disrupted', not because we exist corporeally, but because we are tied to a corporality still alien to us. And this 'strangeness' of our corporality comes as it were, not from our body, but from the powerlessness of our soul, which has lost the vitality that came from grace and is therefore incapable of fully mastering the body. We shall try to elucidate this in three points.

Limitation of life

Man did not select his body, but received it—with all its advantages and disadvantages—from his parents. Through birth, man was—so to speak—'thrust into' a community, which imposed on him the overwhelmingly greater part of his ideas, feelings, values and reactions. A bundle of modes of action, 'determined in advance', arose in him during the first years of his education; these reach deep down into the unconscious. Psychological complications, to be borne throughout his whole life, were then fixed in him. Prejudices, standards of value, modes of behaviour, were—one might say—'instilled' into him. These 'instillations' took on in his existence the form of mechanisms of action.

Thus there slowly emerged a 'foreign material', out of which he was expected to begin to form his 'person'. But since his spirit no longer possesses the vitality which comes from grace, he is incapable of making this foreign body 'his own'. That is why his corporality circumscribes life itself in him ('limitation of life'). He can never quite overcome the strangeness, the heaviness and opacity of his body. He simply lacks the strength for this. That is why he remains a stranger also in the world: a stranger to things, persons and events. But above all he is and remains 'alien' to himself. August Brunner says:

> Through his aversion from God, in whose creative love lies the reason for his existence and for his existing person-ally, man has been twisted and has largely lost his original

power so to make soul penetrate body and to take this over
into his own personal existence that it would follow perfectly and without resistance every impulse of the spirit.
Separated through its own fault from the proper ground of
its existence, the existent being has no longer any firm
centre. In the self therefore lies the true and most profound
reason for self-estrangement. The inertia, impenetrability
of the body and its opposition to the spirit is merely a consequence of this, not its cause. . . . Matter and body, no less
than spirit, proceed from God's creating hand and therefore cannot possibly be evil in themselves. Thus the cause
of self-estrangement must lie in the spirit, which is too
weak to raise the body up to itself. . . . Salvation therefore
is not liberation from the body, but liberation of the body
through the liberation and restoration of the spirit. . . . Man
therefore must be redeemed in order to come to himself.
He must be bent to God to enable his return to God to be
what it ought to be. He must be brought back again to
God, to the source of his being, in order to find himself.
By loving obedience to God and practical love for men, in
the darkness of faith and the pain of apparent self-abandon-
ment, the return of man to himself is invisibly prepared.
The focal point of his being is shifted more and more
decisively towards the centre at which he is really himself,
until in glory it becomes clear what it means to be redeemed: that he has found his way home to himself,
because through love he has found his way home to God,
the source of his own being.

Loss of all-cosmic presence

Our present corporality, not wholly penetrable by the
spirit, not only creates for man a limitation of life, but
leads to a 'spatial limitation' being imposed on him.
That is to say: man does not simply stand there, as if
'fallen from heaven', but is in fact deeply involved in the
world around him, that world out of which God's hand

raised him. Furthermore, a cosmic history is fulfilled in man. Man and the universe are bound together in a single destiny. As 'microcosm', man is a 'compendium' of the universe. Therefore the true 'home' of man—however strange this may sound—ought to be the universe in all its dimensions.

It must be remembered also that the spirit-soul is a 'spirit-become-body', an 'immateriality tied to the body'. But it is proper to the spirit, not to be 'thrown back' on to a limited part of the universe. Of itself the spirit ought to be able to traverse three-dimensional space, to be everywhere at the same time, that is 'all-cosmic'. This capacity of being present to the whole cosmos the spirit-soul has lost, because it 'fell away' from the presence of God that fills the whole universe. Thus it has been thrown back on the spatial limitation of the body, instead of elevating its body to all-cosmic presence. Only when the human spirit in an absolutely whole-hearted decision finds its way back again to God can it fill the world, can it set aside its present 'spatial limitation' and be wholly 'present to the world' and also 'extend' the body to the dimensions of the universe. Only then does man begin to live in accordance with his true nature.

Temporal succession instead of permanence

The incapacity of the spirit to bring the body wholly under its domination leads also to a 'temporal limitation' of our person. The spirit wholly tied to corporality (that is, not recasting the body) lives 'materially' in a succession of moments of time. Its life is—so to speak—split into innumerable flashes of existence. It enters into existence only at each single moment. But this length of time is not sufficient for the realization of all the riches

of the human spirit. Properly speaking then, man 'is' not
yet: he is constantly becoming. He cannot live in an un-
divided present. Only at the moment when the spirit has
found its way back wholly to God, to God who lives his
life from eternity to eternity in a single present, can there
lie open to it a new dimension of duration: a duration in
which man no longer lives in 'bits' of time. Only then
does a life 'worthy of man' begin for us, a life consisting
of a constant, unceasing present.

In his resurrection, Christ overcame all these restrictions on human existence. In him, man in his true reality
became visible. Hence our meditation must be concentrated on Christ, the Risen One. In him we shall discover
in what form of existence world-reality reaches its consummation.

THE CONSUMMATION OF THE BODY IN THE RISEN CHRIST

When we read carefully the Gospel accounts of the risen
Christ, we find there an element of strangeness. The restrictions of corporality no longer exist for Christ: he
appears, suddenly comes alongside the two disciples, disappears, passes through closed doors. A new mode of
existence, incomprehensible in earthly terms, has now
emerged: human reality is transformed. The limits of
time and space have fallen away. Matter has become
wholly spirit. This Christ is radiant with all the colours
and lights of beauty. His being illumines the world as
far as the outermost spheres. His brow is the brightness
of the sun, his eyes are fire; his form sparkles more than
melting gold; his hands hold captive the stars. He has
become the First and the Last, the Living One. His resur-

rection was not simply a return to his previous life—as, for instance, was the raising of Lazarus, who lived again under the restrictions of our existence. Christ's resurrection is in fact a transfiguration.

A new form of existence

John described this form of existence in the introductory vision of his 'Revelation':

> I turned to see the voice that was speaking to me, and on turning I saw seven golden lampstands, and in the midst of the lampstands one like a son of man, clothed with a long robe and with a golden girdle round his breast; his head and his hair were white as white wool, white as snow; his eyes were like a flame of fire, his feet were like burnished bronze, refined as in a furnace, and his voice was like the sound of many waters; in his right hand he held seven stars, from his mouth issued a sharp two-edged sword, and his face was like the sun shining in full strength. When I saw him, I fell at his feet as though dead (Rev. 1. 12–17).

It is of this Christ that the Apostle Paul says: 'The Lord is spirit' (cf. 2 Cor. 3.17). In this sentence, the word 'spirit' does not mean distinction from corporality. It means: raised above the restrictions of earthly existence, taken up into eternity, into life, space and time without bounds. 'Spirit' here means the whole existence, in so far as it has become luminous, in so far as it exists as shining light, creative force, holy vitality, intensity of reality, as glory, in so far as man has become a shining flame of pure reality.

The human countenance remains for eternity

After accomplishing his work of redemption, the Son of God did not cease to be man. The human countenance remains for eternity the countenance of God. On this countenance we see all the things and events of earth as it were melted into one; the whole world has become eternally one in the glow of divinity. That is the last possible word on God and on the world. Human existence has climbed beyond the outermost sphere of the world and entered into the life of the Holy Trinity. Therein the world reached its final consummation, returned to the womb from which it emerged in time immemorial.

Christ is the 'first-born of creation', the 'first fruits', the 'beginning', the 'primal reason of the world' (cf. Col. 1.15–18). In him the world was raised up into the external existence of God. In world-reality therefore he is the indestructible beginning. He penetrates our world-sphere as blazing heat. All is to be taken up into him. In Christ the world entered upon its true state. In him the universe reaches its consummation. The world is already redeemed. It is eternal. But we human beings have to achieve our eternity, we have to take our body into the final consummation. For we human beings can become 'eternal' only through our free decision. By the fact of deciding for Christ, by entering with him into a unity of love and existence, we gain the unity of our being as intended by God, the glory of our soul and of our body. Only in this way do we become 'men'.

MAN'S RISEN BODY

What is man's risen body? Before answering this question, we would like to raise another: one concerned apparently with a secondary problem, but which will lead us very close to the essential definition of the risen body. We know that the argument here set out will seem overbold to many. Nevertheless, we would like to formulate it as a hypothesis, as a starting-point therefore to reflection, which we would think out afresh at any time or even entirely abandon if faced by better counter-arguments.

When does our resurrection take place?

On the one hand, revelation insists that the resurrection is an event coming at the end of time: 'with the archangel's call, and with the sound of the trumpet of God...the dead in Christ will rise first' (1 Thess. 4.16). This is the first factor which we must recognize unconditionally: man's resurrection coincides with Christ's return at the end of time. On the other hand, we must also reflect on the fact that a state of severance from the body is utterly unnatural for the soul. We have observed that the spirit-soul, by its very nature as soul, is involved from the beginning in an immediate relationship to matter. Is God supposed to hold back the soul artificially from every bodily contact, after death, until the resurrection at the end of time? Such an idea would be just as bizarre as an attempt to keep alive by artificial breathing a person who can breathe in a perfectly normal way. This is the second factor, which we must also clearly recognize. By natural necessity the soul impresses its essence on matter and therefore cannot exist for a single moment without the body.

Karl Rahner tries to unite these two factors in a single hypothesis, which is very attractive if not entirely satisfying.[1] He comes to the conclusion that the 'separation of

[1] *On the Theology of Death* (translated by Charles H. Henkey), Herder, Freiburg; Burns & Oates, 5th imp. 1964, especially pp. 24–34.

body and soul' in death does not mean a complete 'break-
away' from matter, but—on the contrary—that precisely
through death's occurrence there arises for the soul a new
and essential closeness to matter. If we try to define the
nature of this closeness, it becomes clear that the human
soul in death, instead of becoming 'a-cosmic' (out of the
world), enters into a new relationship with materiality:
that it therefore becomes in a real sense (although difficult to define) 'all-cosmic' (everywhere present in the
world). This new relationship would place the soul at
that point where all the nature of the world grows up out
of the grounds of its own being. Death accordingly
would be the descent to the matrix of the world, to the
original unity of reality, where everything is linked together at the centre, where all things are living as at their
root: to the last, deepest and most essential reality. Such
a relation to the world means that the soul, when it has
given up its circumscribed bodily shape and thus lies open
in death to the universe, becomes present in some way to
the whole world—indeed, that it takes part in shaping
and determining the events of the universe from their
ultimate source.

We might describe this central point of the world with
the primitive word 'heart'. In death, the soul reaches the
'heart of the universe'. In this hypothesis we can then
better explain Christ's 'descent into hell'. The human
soul of Christ in the 'descent into hell', in its 'descent into
the depths of the earth', would have entered into an open,
unrestricted relationship to the world-whole. The whole
world would thereby have become the 'corporeal organ'
of Christ; and Christ could thus directly act upon all
men, indeed on all beings which belong corporeally to
our cosmos.

This all-cosmic relation to the world of the spirit-soul that has passed through death is not an idea which can be rejected *a priori* as inconceivable, however difficult it may be to define more exactly in terms of our traditional philosophical-theological conceptual system and however little our categories are adapted to it. All we are asking is: why stick at this interpretation and why not venture on a much more radical advance into the mystery of the resurrection?

With Christ's resurrection, the state of resurrection was in principle extended to all men. The Last Day has already dawned. Why could the resurrection not take place at once, at death? There is only one argument—but a very weighty one—which seems to count against such an assumption: the express statements of revelation to the effect that the resurrection will take place only at the end of time. We must not 'demythologize', 'restrict' these statements of revelation about the 'Last Day' or permit them to be 'distorted'.

Here is our suggested solution. The resurrection takes place at once as we pass through death; but it is not yet perfect. The risen body needs the transformed, glorified cosmos as its sphere of being. We can experience our resurrection-corporality in its full realization only when the world has entered into the state of glory. The glorious transformation of the world at the end of time would also be the final perfection of the resurrection which already occurred at death. Thus both statements are appropriate: the resurrection is realized immediately at death—the resurrection is a consequence of the ending of time.

After these reflections, we can raise the essential ques-

4

tion: what really is the risen body? We must answer quite
honestly: we do not know. We know only that the risen
body will be the perfect expression of a spirit-soul eternally united with God. From this starting-point we are
able to say at least what that body cannot be.

A body without suffering

The risen body cannot experience any suffering. It is
wholly taken up into the spirit, into a spirit which is
entirely with God, living in infinite, bliss. Resurrection
therefore means first of all impassibility. This is one of
the themes in the New Testament which constantly recur
in connection with eternal glory. The elect are com-
forted; they are satisfied; God himself will wipe every
tear from their eyes; death will be no more, nor distress,
nor hardship; the sun will no longer scorch, nor will
there be any burning heat (cf. Rev. 7.16–17; 21.4).

But in the Bible this impassibility is merely the obverse
of an enrichment with infinite gifts. Man will shine like
the sun in the kingdom of the Father. God said: 'It is
done. . . . To the thirsty I will give water without price
from the fountain of the water of life. He who conquers
will have this heritage, and I will be his God and he shall
be my son' (Rev. 21.6–7). And finally the mysterious
promise symbolizing our dominion over the universe: 'He
who conquers and who keeps my works until the end,
. . . I will give him the morning star' (Rev. 2.26, 28). God
therefore will penetrate completely man's whole nature,
body and soul, and will shine through all the pores of
human existence.

Experiencing God with all the senses

Our body's estrangement from God will completely

cease in the risen state. Corporality will be taken over into the immediate experience of God. With all our senses we shall experience God.

Ignatius of Loyola in his *Exercises* teaches how man already in his earthly life can attain to an inward 'feeling and tasting' of the Godhead. Augustine in his *Confessions*[2] describes the closeness of God in terms of sensible experience:

> But what do I love, when I love thee? Not the body's grace, nor time's glory; not the brightness of light, pleasing to these eyes; not the sweet melodies of all kinds of songs; not the fragrance of flowers, ointments and spices; not manna and honey; not members made for fleshly embraces: these are not what I love when I love my God. And yet I do love a light, a melody, a fragrance, a food, an embrace, when I love my God: light, melody, fragrance, food, embrace of my inward man; here shines on my soul what place does not hold; and here sounds what time does not snatch away; and here is a fragrance that the wind does not disperse; here is a flavour that voracity does not diminish; and here clings what satiety does not destroy. This is what I love, when I love my God.

Origen says:

> The blessed prophets discovered the divine sensuousness. They gazed in a divine way and heard in a divine way; and they tasted and perceived—if I might say so—by means of an unsensuous sensitivity, feeling the Word by faith, so that it streamed upon them like a healing rain.

These experiences anticipate the condition of the risen body, in which all this will reach its full development.

Present in the glory of the world

The body will no longer be a restrictive factor. The

---

[2] Book X, vi. 8. Translation is from the Latin, owing something to the author's German rendering and Pusey's English (Everyman, 1907). —*Translator.*

spirit, roused by grace to true and lasting life, will be able to be 'itself' in the body. The body's touch will be a spiritual act: tasting, seeing, smelling and hearing, likewise. There will be an end, too, of all that strenuous elaboration of sense-impressions by which our spirit advances from nerve-stimulations and the diversity of its experiences to the invisible source of reality. Seeing becomes intuition; touching, knowing; hearing, understanding; tasting, complete awareness; smelling, loving. The bounds of space will fall away: the spirit will exist immediately at the point to which its love, longing and happiness draw it. There will no longer be anything unattainable. And this intuitive presence of the human soul in the whole world will have that sweetness and warmth which comes from the earthiness of our senses and which —when man has once experienced it—is to endure for ever. Is there anyone among us who would like to live purely 'spiritually'? Who would want to lose all that is involved in the view of a flowering meadow, in the embrace of someone we love, in the sound of a pleasing voice, in tasting satisfying food and in smelling a pleasant, 'beautiful' fragrance?

In this respect the angels really deserve our 'compassion'. They have no 'heart'. Particularly 'this heart is the mystery of being man, deeper, more abysmal, more spacious than all that is "purely spiritual", spiritually flowering...yet always confined to the solid and deep abyss of life's isolation' (G. Siewerth). The centre-point of the world is not an angel, but risen man: he is the unity and peak of all nature, the supreme vital union of all cosmic relations, the mingling and uniting together of all contrasts and elements.

Risen man is the loveliest child of earth and at the same

time a being in which God reposes. In him the universe reaches its eternal consummation, so that Schelling could say: 'It has become absolutely clear to me and penetrated deeply into my heart that we are children of nature, that by our first birth we belong to her and that we can never wholly cut loose from her; that if she does not belong to God, neither can we belong to him; and if she cannot become one with God, then our union with him also must either be imperfect or even impossible.'

Never before was the body taken so seriously and given such absolute reverence as in Christianity. Who could grasp the unfathomable depths of Paul's words, that the Holy Spirit is sent out 'into our hearts' (Gal. 4.6) and that our body (not our spirit) is a 'temple of the Holy Spirit' (I Cor. 6.19)? And finally what more profound utterance about human nature could there be than the revelation that the womb of a virgin is a more noble shrine of God than the bright, luminous expanse of a pure spirit?

In the light of this understanding of our created being and of our corporality, we shall now answer (as far as this is possible) in the three following meditations the agonizing questions of sickness, suffering and death. Then in a final meditation we shall try to press on to the real mystery of our body-soul reality: to the mystery of eternal life.

III

SICKNESS

THE first requirement of Christian love of neighbour is to resist all evil in the world. It is our most Christian duty to spare those we love—and we have an obligation to love as many people as possible—everything that might depress and hurt them: that is, we must make their way easier to eternal bliss, to heaven. This holds above all for sickness. As long as resistance is possible, the Christian will defy it. The Christian must be united with God in the fight against evil. Christian life is built on our 'neighbour'. As a Christian, I have to help my forsaken and suffering brother and by that very fact I am a Christian. A Christianity which evades the urgent duties of love for the poorest and the forsaken is sheer hypocrisy.

Let us first hear an account from the Gospel:

Jesus went up to Jerusalem. Now there is in Jerusalem by the Sheep Gate a pool, in Hebrew called Bethzatha, which has five porticoes. In these lay a multitude of invalids, blind, lame, paralysed. One man was there, who had been ill for thirty-eight years. When Jesus saw him and knew that he had been lying there a long time, he said to him, 'Do you want to be healed?' The sick man answered him, 'Sir, I have no man to put me into the pool when the water is troubled, and while I am going another steps down before me.' Jesus said to him, 'Rise, take up your pallet, and walk.' And at once the man was healed, and he took up his pallet and walked (John 5.1-9).

It is one of the most terrible experiences in a man's life to have to complain: 'I have no one.' As long as a person in my neighbourhood, in a group to which I have access, has to say that, I am not a Christian. My eternal happiness depends on my understanding the words of Christ:

> Come, O blessed of my Father, inherit the kingdom prepared for you from the foundation of the world; for I was hungry and you gave me food, I was thirsty and you gave me drink, I was a stranger and you welcomed me, I was naked and you clothed me, I was sick and you visited me, I was in prison and you came to me (Matt. 25.34–36).

These are certainly not 'symbolic expressions'. They must be understood in their stern reality. Of course, spiritual distress, mental captivity, spiritual hunger, are also stern realities. But anyone who never in his life gave food to a hungry person, never offered drink to a thirsty man, never sheltered a stranger, clothed the naked, visited the sick, consoled a prisoner, will certainly not enter heaven: inwardly therefore he is not a Christian, he has grasped nothing of the essence of Christianity. He has passed reality by.

Man becomes a Christian, not primarily by attaining ecstasy in prayer, nor because he knows a lot about commandments and prohibitions, but by selflessly ministering to his forsaken brother in ordinary life, his brother who until then had to say: 'I have no one.' The person who goes out and helps a poor, sick man, or merely someone who feels that he is forsaken, will one day hear the words of Christ: 'Blessed are you. From the beginning of the world, I prepared a kingdom for you: heaven. You were a Christian.'

But who is my neighbour? When Christ was asked this, he did not give an abstract definition, but told a story: the story of the Good Samaritan. The essential point of this story is this: my neighbour is the one whom no one will help if I don't. My neighbour is that person who has me alone to help him. The whole approach of the Christian to salvation is this: Do what no one else will do in your place; hold yourself ready, become open-hearted, be accessible to every kind of suffering. If this is your outlook, you will one day meet the person who has no one but you. Then you must accept your destiny. Stay there: do not pass by; bend down.

Blessed—that is, worthy of heaven—is the one who has ministered to his brother, who has taken to himself the other's misery, who spent himself, belittled himself in service and devotion. God's first move is to spare us injuries, to bind up wounds. The more we relieve the suffering of others at every moment, with our whole heart and with all our strength, so much the closer do we come to the heart of Christ. God expects us to fight against evil and not to give up this struggle. As a Christian—and, indeed, by the very fact that I exist—I may not abandon the fight before all possibilities are exhausted. Otherwise Christianity really would be an opium for the people. Otherwise we would not reshape suffering, but succumb to it. There is an anger, a holy wrath which God feels towards evil. In this spirit of genuinely Christian anger, we ought to set ourselves against evil in the world.

God wants us to help him. He has not 'spirited away' distress, out of our life. The Christian suffers, hungers, fights and dies like all other human beings. But for him

suffering, hunger, struggle and death have acquired
quite another meaning. They are to provide for him the
chance of passing through suffering to God, of fleeing
from darkness into light. In reality, the solution is quite
simple. God has permitted us to fall into need, so that in
trying to escape it we may take refuge in him, so that he
can bestow on us—God-estranged beings—his closeness,
eternal bliss, heaven.

It is the function of the Christian in the world to transform darkness into light: if we are sick, to lie there; to
endure our body's misery and allow ourselves to be carried up by it into bliss. We ought really to be happy if
we are able to suffer in a Christian way. This means
banishing suffering from the world: we take it on ourselves, destroy it and thus enter on the way of eternal
happiness. To bear suffering and sickness patiently is a
truly Christian duty. The final harvest of being takes
place on the Cross. Suffering endured is the way to the
world's spiritualization. If we want to transform the
world into heaven, we must take to ourselves the misery
and cares of men, so that they are 'taken out', banished
from the world. To suffer, and thereby to be convinced
that we are advancing to an eternal happiness, is a Christian vocation.

Thus the life of the Christian is one continuous joy:
we have an answer even for our worst distress, for our
bodily sickness and our suffering as creatures. For us they
are not a menace, but a charge. The bodily misery of
mankind borne out in a Christian spirit reduces the level
of suffering in the world. If we take suffering on ourselves, we save others from disaster: we bring heaven
closer to the world.

From this reasoning we are led to consider more closely two fundamental virtues: compassion and devotion.

CHRISTIAN COMPASSION

The sick person is a gift of God to us, a direct grace; and as such he must be accepted by us. He is a grace of God to us mainly by giving us the chance to realize that open-heartedness which is known as compassion. Without the virtue of compassion, the world would break down. For without it, it would be difficult or even impossible to attain to that genuine selflessness, to that attitude to reality, in which alone man becomes 'himself'. When we meet the sick person with true Christian compassion, we are performing a deed that is far more than mere sympathy or a little kindness: we are realizing genuine humanity in the world, in fact, we are creating true humanity in ourselves; thus carrying on the evolution of milliards of years. By the virtue of compassion man creates himself in us and through us.

To be compassionate—and not merely occasionally when moved by impulse, but in principle, as an established way of life—requires great power of self-detachment. The only way to acquire this is to become absolutely detached down to the very roots of our nature. This detachment comprises three essential factors, which show us why compassion is a very difficult—indeed, a heart-rending—virtue and why its exercise is precisely what brings about the perfection of human nature: they are poverty, chastity and obedience. It should be observed, however, that we are not discussing here the special vows of the religious state, but those virtues of the heart to which every Christian is called—whether he is a religious or not.

Spiritual poverty

Compassion is essentially an attitude of poverty. It enters into a unity of existence with a suffering being, lays itself open to another's suffering, not because it has to do this, but because it is inwardly gripped by suffering that is not its own. The compassionate man is not intent upon his own security. He is not chained to himself. He frees himself in order to be able to enter into another's need. He creates an open space within himself. In his own eyes, he himself no longer counts. He makes himself utterly small, does not seek his own advantage, gives himself defencelessly and without question, loses himself in the other. His life is a realization of our Saviour's mode of existence, of the dispositions described in the Epistle to the Philippians:

> Have this mind among yourselves, which was in Christ Jesus, who, though he was in the form of God, did not count equality with God a thing to be grasped, but emptied himself, taking the form of a servant, being born in the likeness of men. And being found in human form he humbled himself (Phil. 2.5-8).

Only such dispositions make man personally and spiritually creative. A person like this will not 'dominate' the world. He holds himself open to whatever God may send him: joy, suffering, burdens, relief, past and future. With such a person God can really do what he wills. He has made himself 'receptive'. He has learned that reality in the last resort is grace. Indeed, he has learned still more: he knows now that this attitude itself—being able to open himself, to create in himself an emptiness, a state of poverty—is ultimately a gift.

This complete openness towards all life's events—whether they are beneficial or even life-consuming—demands effort, victory over sloth, over our own self-satisfaction. Man must renounce his own rest and his own peace, constantly tear himself away from himself. This is the attitude known as 'poverty of spirit'. In its deliberate, spiritual realization it is also 'receptivity' in regard to the world. In it there is concentrated the great tension of the universe awaiting the gift of glory: 'the bright Credo of the suns, the Gloria of the stars, earth pregnant with flowers offering love's prayers' (Gertrud von le Fort). Anyone who lives out humanly—and therefore heartily and joyously—this radical openness of being towards the sick and miserable creature is compassionate.

Chastity

Compassion is just as essentially an attitude of chastity. The virtue of which we are speaking here is not a negative quality, the crippling or denial of life. Chastity is pure positivity of being: the straightforwardness, the ardour, which makes love capable of really loving. From this standpoint, 'impure', 'unchaste' would be terms applied to that being which is 'wrapped up' in egoism, which is self-seeking, unloving. Purity is realized in a person whose own ego does not stand in the forefront of his consciousness, whose vital impulses 'go out' from him, for whom others stand at the centre of his life, who turns absolute detachment and openness of existence into deeds, who completely 'pulls himself together' and gives himself without reserve, who no longer 'looks back' at himself, but commits himself with his entire personal reality.

Chastity of existence is nothing but the devotion of a person who is 'whole', wholly serving, wholly upright.

Such devotion practically 'forces' God to enter into the world, to bestow himself on the world. Therein lies the mystery of the Annunciation. 'When the moment came at which God had decided to realize the Incarnation before our eyes, he had first to arouse in the world a virtue which was capable of drawing him down to us. . . . He created the Virgin Mary: that is, he made so great a purity arise on earth that he could embody himself in this transparency until he appeared as a small child' (Teilhard de Chardin). The holy Virgin was the density of life. In her was concentrated the vitality of the universe. She made 'life', Christ, come forward; Christ who leads us and the universe into the ultimate fullness of life. In Christ, then, being flashed out. The disciples had a shattering experience of this brightness, this intensification of reality, this metamorphosis of being into glory:

> He was transfigured before them, and his face shone like the sun, and his garments became white as light (Matt. 17.2).

A message of pure vitality. This is chaste existence, transparency out of true reality. In a chaste person life ought to shine out. In him there ought to occur what the Acts of the Apostles records of the deacon, Stephen:

> Gazing at him, all who sat in the council saw that his face was like the face of an angel (Acts 6.15).

Genuine love says 'Yes', without reserve, to the beloved 'thou'. So much so that it does not want to 'use up' the other, demanding nothing from it. Thus a truly burning love becomes pure affirmation of the other being, which —precisely because we love it—we will not treat as a 'possession'. This glowing presence of love, this pure giving, this absolute devotion, is existential chastity: it can be realized, not only in the state of virginity, but also in that of marriage. It is an attitude of respect, of consideration and fine restraint, which must be involved even in the sexual act where spiritual love finds bodily expression, if this is to reach its perfection.

Anyone who brings this thoroughgoing devotion to all creatures—therefore also to the sick, the suffering and the infirm—is compassionate. It exhausts him, brings him to the end of his resources, but at the same time raises the world closer and closer to the light.

Obedience

Compassion, by its very nature, is an attitude of obedience. It is an assent to being absolutely, in whatever form this may present itself: healthy or sick, exciting or boring, stimulating or dull. Human reality is free in the proper sense only when it no longer seeks what might satisfy itself, but what brings happiness and fulfilment to others; when it becomes so independent that it no longer clings to itself. Such a freedom, going beyond itself, is realized in obedience towards being: in that freedom wants to do nothing but serve, be at the disposal of others, give the heart; it will not thrust itself forward, will no longer exist for itself. Such freedom is spontaneous love, promptly given; it is the power of a heart stirred by the good.

A great tenderness for being lies in this freedom. Complete detachment. Pure readiness. A readiness that is wholly receptivity towards the new. It is a sign that the soul is still young, that it can go on to a still greater fulfilment, that there is nothing in it to hinder the advent of what is greater than itself. This freedom is the spirit's youth, the joy within it, its capacity for transformation. Such a freedom assents to all that is. In it man's nature opens out: there emerges a new expanse into which God's being can enter and in which a second creation, the new creation, begins.

The proclamation of this miracle was our Lord's deepest concern: the miracle of a new world coming to be. There has been nothing so free as that love with which Christ sought the will of the Father. Christ did not work out any plan of life, did not announce any programme, was not preoccupied with his own fate. He was free: open to the moment and to the needs of others revealed in that moment. He let himself be led. What was realized in him is remotely prefigured in Psalm 131 (130, Vulgate):

> O Lord, my heart is not lifted up,
> my eyes are not raised too high;
> I do not occupy myself with things
> too great and too marvellous for me.
> But I have calmed and quieted my soul,
> like a child quieted at its mother's breast,
> like a child that is quieted is my soul

Christ submitted himself completely to his destiny, which was never an anonymous fate, but the will of the Father.

A person who realizes this attitude says to himself: Go to God; he will lead you out of your confinement, thus he will lead you into eternity; you will be constantly becoming new; your freedom becomes perfect when you give yourself to your God; heaven arises in the world only when you give God space in your being. In compassionate love for the broken creature, man practises for the greatest obedience that he can accomplish towards being. He accepts God's will, completely: even when this

will appears to be meaningless and to make excessive
demands.

Compassion as radical assent to the creature

Compassion is the peak of true human reality. In it
our nature 'bursts out', without reserve; it opens itself
out to an infinite fulfilment; to a fulfilment which calls
forth a constant vacuum so that man's nature can be
filled still more (poverty). In it man becomes open, only
giving himself and expecting nothing in return, therefore wholly 'going away' from himself (chastity). In it
is implied an assent to infinity, to the infinite fulfilment
which constantly fills us and disposes of us; it is a commitment of oneself to otherness (obedience).

Compassion then is not a special virtue, but an epitome
of all the virtues of the heart, of which heaven is built
up. And these in turn are not diverse virtues, but the
single quality of love: of a love which has become devotion and which precisely in this devotion reaches its
absolute fulfilment. In compassion man annihilates himself, gives his being unreservedly, bestows himself disinterestedly on anyone he meets. Thus human reality
becomes perfect. (In this sense, the evangelical counsels
of poverty, chastity and obedience are valid for every
Christian and admit of no exception.) The atmosphere,
the field of existence surrounding the Christian—whose
life is seen to be compassion without reserve—becomes
ever more luminous, ever more 'charged' with God.

The glowing testimony of compassion brings about a
concentration of the divine in our world. An immense
power is concealed in it, the power of the divine presence
in the world. The world has—so to speak—sent the com-

passionate man in advance, to prepare the way for mankind. He takes the life of the world with him into the breath-taking adventure of union with God. He drags the others after him. A tremendous responsibility lies upon him. He belongs no longer to himself, but to mankind. He is a gift of God to the world. Man's assent to the creature is nowhere so radically expressed as in the virtue of compassion.

But compassion can be perfect only if it is practised joyfully. The more we take as God's gift to us an exhausted human being precisely in his exhaustion, the more we help him to bear his suffering, so much the more do we turn earth into heaven, so much the more do we give the world the possibility of union with happiness— that is, with God—and of reaching perfection. If anyone truly deserves to be called happy, it is the person to whom God sends one in need of his compassion. God has chosen him to live a life of selfless, unremitting devotion and thus to maintain intact the human reality in mankind, to lead earth to heaven, to be creation's pilot.

CHRISTIAN DEVOTION

In what does the Christian vocation of a sick man consist? First of all, let us express the answer in an utterly simple way: the Christian's function is to overcome the darkness of the world, to open the way for light and joy to descend upon the world. Every Christian is called to do this. The world is full of darkness, gloom, confusion, obscurity. When a Christian receives God's grace to enable him to gather up this darkness into his existence, he can then be certain of his election. God has destined him to gather to himself what is burdensome, dark and heavy out of the world and to translate it into

5

divine joy. He has the duty of opening wide his soul, of letting all suffering flow into it. If he does this, his own soul will become darker and darker, but the world around him clearer, more serene. When he lays himself open to the light of the Godhead, this darkness disappears, his soul becomes clear and radiant. By gathering to himself the darkness of the earth and opening his existence to the light of Christ, he has made the world happier, he has brought it a step nearer heaven.

To anyone who has grasped this there is nothing—nothing at all—more that needs saying on the mystery of human suffering. Such a person thanks the Lord whenever he is allowed to suffer. He sees that God has chosen him to endure what others can no longer bear. Sick people, bearing their sickness as Christians, are our salvation: they give us the chance of living in light, of abandoning ourselves to joy. Someone must bear the world's suffering so that others may have it easier. If you are that one, then thank your Lord every day for being allowed to suffer, for being able to share in his work of redeeming the world. Suffering is election. God grant us the opportunity of suffering and in addition his grace, so that we may bear it in a Christian way.

Let us now develop this first answer in two points.

Devotion as spiritualization of the world

Human life does not run on one plane. The one way of life exists at different levels. On the higher plane other systems of meaning hold. Kierkegaard expressed this clearly in his work, *Stages on Life's Way*. The man who lives his life 'ahead' suddenly comes to a brink. He says to himself: 'On this plane of my being, in this order of existence, I have "outlived" myself. If my life is not radically altered now, my true reality will be shrivelled up. I must venture into darkness, into what has not yet been explored.' At first obscurely, but then constantly more clearly and urgently, man becomes aware that something higher awaits him, not to be attained by a gradual approach and transition, but only by a choice and a leap.

Human existence truthfully lived, therefore, consists of existential planes and the ventures which lie before each plane. Augustine, for example, was impelled by the death of a young friend to the decisive leap of his life. Buddha experienced the suffering of the world in a moment of spiritual clairvoyance: he stood up and went—as it is reported—'out into homelessness'. The occasion of the greatest venture of Pascal's life was a mystical experience described in his *Memorial*. Often it is sickness or the breakdown of a life's work, or even the death of someone we loved, that gives us the decisive impulse for the 'leap in the dark'. If we were never to go through such experiences of times of crisis for body and soul, our life would become stagnant. When a hurt, an upheaval, suffering, impel us to reach a higher plane of existence, then we must say of these things that they were at the service of life. In a way, that may hold also for sin. In view of sinners who became saints, of an Augustine, a Magdalen or a Lydwina,[1] we do not hesitate for a

[1] Lydwina,' born 1380 at Schiedam, near Rotterdam, was as a girl much admired for her beauty. After breaking a rib through falling on ice, she spent thirty-eight years heroically bearing the most appalling illnesses which disfigured her utterly. During that time she had many visions and ecstasies. She died in 1433. Her feast is kept on 14 April. She is honoured in many places as patroness of the sick and of the apostolate to the sick. For a full account of her life the reader is referred to Hubert Meuffels, *Sainte Lydwine* (1925).—*Translator.*

moment to say *felix culpa,* 'sin bringing happiness'. Not because sin in itself ceases to be sin, but because they knew how to use it—so to speak—as a springboard from which to leap to God.

Teilhard de Chardin, a man who knew from personal experience a great deal about the depths of misery, sickness, lack of success, and bodily and mental breakdown, wrote an introduction to a book of drawings by his sister who had lain a lifetime seriously ill. There he says:

> Margaret, my sister! While I—devoted to the positive forces of the universe—was traversing continents and oceans, passionately concerned to see all the colours and beauties of the earth, you were lying there, stretched out motionless, transforming in your innermost being the worst darknesses of the world into light. In the sight of God, our Creator—tell me—which of us two had the better part?

We must firmly maintain that human life 'goes ahead' only when it is thrust out of the state it has already reached through suffering and distress and ventures to break out of its littleness. May God protect us from those people who were always successful in life, who never had to cry out their despair into the world, who never felt the apparent senselessness and peril of human life in the extremes of sickness, who never urgently stormed the Lord in prayer to release them from their suffering by death and to take them up into heaven! Such people have not experienced the longing of all longings, do not bear within themselves the pressure of the universe, have never experienced the bliss of that cry for help which lies in the last words of Scripture: 'Come, Lord Jesus!' What hope would be left to our world if it were no longer able to utter through human lips this cry for eternal consummation?

Devotion as self-abandonment

But there is human suffering—and death, particularly, is such—in which man completely breaks down, in which he can experience nothing more, neither longing nor hope. The extreme limit of what can be existentially experienced has been reached. Man can go no further. He would like to be annihilated, to be no more, to have no one remember him any longer. He can no longer master his fate. He cries out: 'My God, my God, why hast thou forsaken me?'

Is there still an answer? Yes: God is the Wholly-Other. And the Wholly-Other begins at the point where we leave off. We can encounter him only at the end of our resources: in that which is folly to the world, unbearable to feeling, meaningless to understanding. Up to that point man might confuse God with something else, with his wishes, with his vitality, with his joy in existence. But at the point where nothing of man remains, God appears in all his purity. Man can finally die 'to' God. He can say: 'I have nothing more, I have no answer, nothing to say. Make of me what you will. If it is your will, annihilate me; your will be done. I want nothing more, can want nothing more.'

What then is this final impotence of the creature? It is the experience of the fact that the truly real transcends all things, all anticipations and all powers. In this final despair of itself, the world becomes utterly open to God. And God can fill it wholly: out of pure mercy. We cannot force God. No one has a right to his grace.

Nevertheless, God 'forced' himself: he let us enter into
absolute powerlessness, so that we should feel irrevocably
lost. This abandonment then rouses God's all-transcend-
ing mercy, and he gives himself boundlessly. No one can
be so sure of God's infinite mercy as the person who has
felt that he was infinitely abandoned and without redemption, who has been nailed to the Cross. The Cross
is the way to the absolutely Other, to that on which man
can no longer call.

We must take care not to rob suffering man of this
precious gift of God by our prattling, not to keep him by
our superficial arguments from totally despairing of himself. That would lead to a situation in which no one any
longer experienced in the world the 'otherness' of God,
no one could any longer receive the total gift. Once
during his life or at least in his death, man must have
experienced that utter exhaustion described by Peter
Lippert:

> You have created oceans of pain ... and I cannot see how
> they were necessary to preserve your world. You went
> ahead with your world-plan, striding across the suffering
> of every single thing, just as you stride across the life of
> individuals. You had your reasons for creating oceans of
> suffering and you did this. You move about these oceans,
> which were formed out of tears. And sometimes these
> oceans rise in stormy tides, striking up at your heaven. ...
> Lord, everything apart from you is plunged in suffering.
> You allow the sea of pain to surge forward up to the steps
> of your throne, to the heights of your majesty; and all that
> goes out from you steps at once into these dark, boiling
> waves. You yourself, when you wanted to descend into the
> world, had to plunge into this ocean of suffering that sur-
> rounds you. Lord, you created pain.
>
> There are some who know everything, who penetrate
> even your great thoughts and decrees and give a nice, tidy

explanation of them all. They explain and prove to me that it has to be just so and is best as it is. But I cannot endure these people who explain everything, who justify and find excuses for everything you do. I prefer to admit that I don't understand. That I cannot grasp why you created pain, why so much pain, such raging, crazy and meaningless pain. I bow down before your glory indeed; but I do not now venture to raise my eyes to you. There is too much grief and weeping in them. So I cannot look on you.

To this finally unendurable state the existence of every believer must come, if he seeks to share in the Wholly-Other. Only there is the world laid open; only there is accomplished the radical ascent in which a new world is created, not by human power, but by the powerlessness of the Cross, drawing to itself the power of God. Teilhard de Chardin expresses it in this way:

This heart-rending eruption from all areas of experience is only the spiritualization of that law which rules all life. To the peaks which for our human eyes are veiled by mists and to those to which the Cross invites us, we climb by a path which is also the track of universal progress. The royal road of the Cross, the road of human effort, oriented and prolonged in a supernatural way. . . . The Cross therefore is not something inhuman, but something super-human. We see that it was erected, from the origin of present-day mankind, on the way that leads to the highest peaks of creation.

To bring out the meaninglessness of a life plunged into pain and nevertheless to see a meaning in this life: that is the Christian answer to the world's suffering. In a word: you must completely lose yourself and then, out of sheer mercy, God gives you something that he would never have given you otherwise. His over-abundant grace consists in confronting you in any event with the possibility of completely despairing of yourself: in death. We shall have to deepen still more this understanding of the world of suffering. In the following meditations we shall turn to that dimension of pain which seizes, not only the body, but the soul: which therefore is not merely pain and sickness, but, in the strictest sense of the word, 'suffering'.

IV

SUFFERING

In the last meditation we were concerned mainly with bodily misery. Now we would like to discuss suffering in the proper sense, our soul's misery. Here, too, the principle of Christian mastery of evil remains the same: we are to spare others everything that might cause them suffering; on the other hand, when it comes before us, we are to take on ourselves mankind's misery, bear it, so that it becomes less and disappears from mankind, so that our world is transformed into heaven.

Christ knew very well the root of our spiritual suffering. In three events he pointed out the way, showed us how to overcome our inner darkness and to win through to his light. We shall discuss here three of our Lord's miracles. Miracles are indeed symbols of a deeper, spiritual reality. Augustine says: 'What our Lord accomplished corporeally, he wanted to be understood spiritually. For he never did miracles for the miracle's sake.' And again: 'He [the centurion] came to ask for the bodily healing of his servant and, as he went away, he had himself gained the kingdom of God.'

OUT OF CLOSENESS TO SELFLESSNESS

The first of these events is recorded in the Gospel in this way:

And they brought to him a man who was deaf and had
an impediment in his speech; and they besought him to
lay his hands upon him. And taking him aside from the
multitude privately, he put his fingers into his ears, and he
spat and touched his tongue; and looking up to heaven, he
sighed, and said to him, 'Ephphatha', that is, 'Be opened.'
And his ears were opened, his tongue was released,
and he spoke plainly. . . . And they were astonished
beyond measure, saying, 'He has done all things well;
he even makes the deaf hear and the dumb speak'
(Mark 7.32–37).

Christ first of all helped this man in the body, but in
addition to this he showed him a way out of spiritual
suffering. He told him: 'Be opened.'

Shrivelled up in self-isolation

At the roots of all our inward decay there lies an
existential closeness, a coldness, an estrangement. Augustine speaks of this condition of human existence in his
commentary on the Psalms: 'Every man is a stranger in
this life. . . . Everyone bears his own heart and every heart
is closed against every other heart.' Man lives in his own
captivity. The sickness of one who cannot hear and cannot speak is only a feeble symbol of an unutterable
spiritual suffering. An armour of ice as it were envelops
us all. We are fettered by chains to ourselves. The first,
immediate reaction of the human heart is to ward off, to
keep at a distance, to distrust. If a man remains stuck in
this, his natural state, he becomes incapable of happiness.
Earth's beauty cannot touch him; he no longer listens to
the melodies of the universe, to human counsel, to the
plea of the suffering. Not even God is able to speak to

him. For speech is complete only in the person who perceives it, understands it, and lays himself open to it.

Enrichment in openness towards being

Existentially to 'listen' to others means to break through our egoism, to turn ourselves away from ourselves, to be 'available' disinterestedly for other people. An absolute openness for being exhausts our nature more than we might at first think, for we live in a world of suffering. In this world, to listen to others, quietly and sympathetically to be 'with them', to let their being flow into us, all this means at the same time: to take on ourselves their confusion, their darkness and their burdens. Existentially to 'speak' to others means in our world: to go out to our fellow-men, to their littleness, to their stupidity; to tell them something useful, not to ourselves, but to them; to accept others with our whole nature. In such 'hearing' and 'talking' a person can utterly exhaust himself. But God did not create us to benefit ourselves: he made us to make something out of ourselves.

In reality, in our world, we have only a single task: to offer a helping hand to our neighbour, to take his fate on ourselves, to enter into the other's misery, to bear another's suffering and thus overcome that suffering. If we do this, we shall have a hard time in the world. But we shall be happy. Even if we are in a state of nervous exhaustion, we shall become wholly a channel for the passage of what is other than ourselves. Our nature will be like an invisible ladder serving the cosmic powers, the angels, as a means of ascending and descending, to bring the world up to God and to bring God down to the world. What we pray for in the Mass will take place in our present existence:

We humbly beseech thee, almighty God, command these offerings to be borne by the hands of thy holy angel to thine altar on high, in the sight of thy divine Majesty.

In a heart absolutely open to God and men (which really means the same thing), heaven and earth coincide.

Hospitality, the sign of an open heart

In this connection a primal virtue of the human heart, 'hospitality', gains a quite special meaning. It is the concrete, living sign of the fact that a person is open to the other being. Of Abraham, the prototype of the true human reality, we read:

> He lifted up his eyes and looked, and behold, three men stood in front of him. When he saw them, he ran from the tent door to meet them, and bowed himself to the earth, and said, 'My lord, if I have found favour in your sight, do not pass by your servant. Let a little water be brought, and wash your feet, and rest yourselves under the tree, while I fetch a morsel of bread, that you may refresh yourselves, and after that you may pass on' (Genesis 18.2-5).

And this visit, as it became clear afterwards, was the visit of God himself.

God is continually coming to us. But his visit always takes the form of a meeting between creatures: three men descended on Abraham, the angel Gabriel on the Virgin, the apostles on the early Christians and often on our door there is only a soft, diffident knocking:

> Behold, I stand at the door and knock; if any one hears my voice and opens the door, I will come in to him and eat with him, and he with me (Rev. 3.20).

Jean Daniélou says: 'If we want the true host, the host in our true home, one day to take us in when we knock—

he has himself told us what we must do. He told us to be ready in this life to open our door to the guest who comes to us. Thus we see what a dignity belongs to hospitality: for our Lord himself makes it the test by which we shall be judged on the Last Day and the key to the lost paradise.'

'God's knocking' symbolizes here a more comprehensive reality: happiness is open to us only if we keep open the doors of our heart, if we are ready to hear and answer, if we do not bolt ourselves in. This is one of the most fundamental requirements of Christianity and Christ's deepest response to spiritual suffering. This answer means simply: Keep yourself ready, give space to others within your being, say at last something good to your fellow-man (no matter how clumsily and awkwardly), and then happiness will one day descend upon you.

FROM STUBBORNNESS TO GRATITUDE

The second event is thus recorded in the Gospel:

> As he entered a village, he was met by ten lepers, who stood at a distance and lifted up their voices and said, 'Jesus, Master, have mercy on us.' When he saw them he said to them, 'Go and show yourselves to the priests.' And as they went they were cleansed. Then one of them, when he saw that he was healed, turned back, praising God with a loud voice; and he fell on his face at Jesus' feet, giving him thanks. . . . Then said Jesus, ... 'Where are the nine?' (Luke 17.12–17).

The misery of the ten directly touched the heart of Christ. He wanted to help them, but in such a way that this help would transform not only their body, but also their whole nature. He succeeded only with one. This shows how

difficult is that which Christ here requires of us: gratitude.

Bitterness in vexation

These men were healed of a very severe illness, leprosy.
In the East at that time lepers were regarded as unclean.
They were thrust out of human society, even out of their
own family. The miraculous cure meant for them
security, new life, family, love and—still more—a lovable-
ness of their own. What we have here are—so to speak—
'professional unfortunates', unfortunates who think they
have a right to compassion and consideration. They are
hard to please, argumentative, complaining, demanding
and accusing. Their life is all bitterness, complaint, pro-
test and demand. Their illness is a sign of their deeper,
spiritual condition: their humanity falls away from
them, bit by bit.

It is as if Christ called to these men: 'If you want to be
happy, be grateful; be a person who does not take for
granted things, gifts, love, friendship and life altogether.
Life itself shrivels up within you, if you want to keep it
only for yourself; if you give nothing away.' The person
who can say, 'Thank you', confesses his own littleness,
admits that he receives his true reality as grace; and precisely in this way he shows that he is more than himself,
that his being is grace.

Liberation in gratitude

It is only in gratitude that man is really redeemed:
redeemed from himself. He is no longer confined to his
small ego. Thus God calls to us: 'Do not be in love with
yourself, with your wretched being: if you were to see

yourself, you would be disgusted with yourself; don't be cramped; I don't want you to be eating your heart out, to have your head constantly in a whirl; you must not be forever concerned with yourself.' Man is grace to such a degree that he must be grateful even for being able to give thanks. Only in such a gratitude reaching to the very roots of being does there arise genuine acceptance, unreserved turning to the other, to the smallest, most obvious thing.

Out of this attitude there grows up a humility towards every kind of creature. The world becomes our sister. Gratitude reconciles man with the universe. There is required from us a universal brotherliness, peaceableness and sympathy, an attitude out of which the new future will emerge. Christian gratitude towards being ought to 'set free' the resources of sympathy slumbering in the depths of the human soul, out of which the new phase of cosmic development results. Truly all things are beneficial to the person who is grateful. He acquires a vital, joyously growing and receptive attitude to life. Only when man gives himself, helps others selflessly, heals them, makes others alive, does he himself become alive. In giving, man becomes a recipient. That is why receiving is the peak of life. True reality cannot be 'achieved', cannot be demanded, cannot be earned. We can only 'let it flow over us'.

The real problem lies in bringing ourselves to such a state of mind that we can hope to find God, a state of mind that is simply: be open, be grateful, go out of your own ego. A man who wants to be man goes beyond himself. The man without 'transcendence', without a 'going out from himself', is de-humanized. We must protect ourselves from ourselves. Our bliss consists in not being able to reach true reality. The failure of our quest for it is our success. Even our quest for God we must accept in gratitude as grace from God's hands and recall that the quest for him always means that he is seeking us. And often he lets himself be found by someone who was not seeking him. The one who accepts nothing with gratitude, receives nothing. The nine lepers who were healed were in fact not healed at the deepest level of their being. They remained 'exposed'.[1] Only the one who returned found fulfilment: in gratitude. We have a right only to what we can receive with gratitude: that is, to that to which in reality we have no right.

FROM ABANDONMENT INTO JOY

The third event is recorded for us in the Gospel of Luke:

> Soon afterwards he went to a city called Nain, and his disciples and a great crowd went with him. As he drew near to the gate of the city, behold, a man who had died was being carried out, the only son of his mother, and she was a widow; and a large crowd from the city was with her. And when the Lord saw her, he had compassion on her and said to her, 'Do not weep.' And he came and touched the bier, and the bearers stood still. And he said, 'Young man, I say to you, arise.' And the dead man sat up and began to speak. And he gave him to his mother (Luke 7.11–15).

Here our Lord released a mother from her despair. He gave back to her all that she had lost.

Christ, our being's assent

Thereby he proved that he—Christ—is *the* answer, the assent of our being. When we think that life is com-

---

[1] *Ausgesetzt,* a play upon the German word for 'leper' (*der Aussätzige*).—*Translator.*

pletely shattered, hopeless, that we have nothing more at
all to which we can cling, then we ought to say to ourselves that Christ one day will give everything back to
us. We ought not to demand any joy, but give it out,
radiate happiness into the world. Even when—humanly
speaking—we are burnt out, we must keep the flame
alive and spread joy to others. Joy can be the heaviest
cross in the life of a Christian. It is the testimony of the
divine that costs perhaps the greatest effort. The harvest
is never 'trodden in'; all hopes are fulfilled. It is only
when we reject God that an ever-widening gap begins to
appear in our life. Only then does our place at the throne
of God remain eternally 'unoccupied'. Even our sin, our
most severe loss, can be made good. God can tell us: 'You
have frustrated my first plans for you. Now I have a new
idea: I shall call you to a new life.'

Outburst into joy

What usually dominates our existence is indolence,
emptiness, aridity and hopelessness. If this is our life, God
can say: 'Stand up!' And then we have to stand up. Then
we must break out again from the dark valleys of our
perishability. That is what happened in the life of the
prophet Elijah. He had to fight a terrible battle, but God
touched him and then everything succeeded with the
greatest ease; afterwards, he lay again on the desert sand
like an exhausted animal until God once more sent him
an angel who raised him up again, beyond human power.
So it goes on until man has completely worn himself out
and goes out again into final aridity and loneliness. And
then comes release. Elijah took a friend with him. But
while they were pressing on into the desert, deep in

conversation, a fiery chariot came and separated them from one another. Elijah was torn away by the whirlwind of fire. Only his prophet's mantle remained, lying on the desert sand.

Still greater things took place in the life of Mary. Karl Rahner describes that life:[2]

> With her as with all the children of this earth, life was a restless coming to be and passing away. Her life began quietly and obscurely, somewhere in a corner of Palestine, and soon it was snuffed out, gently, and the world knew it not. In between these two points, her life was filled with the same restless change that constitutes our life, and it was filled with the cares common to all Eve's children: anxiety for bread, suffering and tears, and a few small joys. So too were her hours measured out to her: a few hours of the utmost happiness in God her Saviour joined with many routine, ordinary hours of grief, one after another, lustreless, feeble, and seemingly so empty and dull. But finally all the hours, the sublime as well as the ordinary, had passed away; and they could all now appear as one insignificant whole, precisely because they could thus fade away into the past.

What took place at the end of this life is utterly inconceivable: it was simply taken up into eternity. Without penance, without having to disown any moment of her existence, she passed over into the eternal house of her glory. Sooner or later that can happen to all of us. Therefore, man, stand up, don't remain there, lying in the desert of your own isolation. Nothing makes your Lord so sad, even wounded in soul, as a Christian who does not live in joy.

Christ broke through our existential closeness and thus

[2] *The Eternal Year* (translated by John Shea), Burns & Oates, London, and Helicon Press, Baltimore, 1964, p. 132.

made possible selflessness, gratitude and joy. Out of these attitudes human happiness emerges. And in them at the same time the world is ascending out of its darkness towards the light.

We shall now try to indicate something of the meaning of the basic existential law, of the fulfilment of existence, by which this essential joy comes to be in us: in what way therefore we can attain to selflessness, gratitude and joy. At the centre of the message of Jesus Christ is the principle of human essentiality: 'He who wants to gain himself must lose himself.' There is no other way to happiness, no other possibility of overcoming suffering, except the radical realization in our life of this basic law of the 'new creation'.

THE BASIC LAW OF HUMAN HAPPINESS

True reality cannot be gained by conquest, but only received as a gift with devotion: a devotion that seeks no advantage and pursues no interest. The refusal of such devotion in principle therefore means self-curtailment. I become 'myself' essentially by giving up myself. Fulfilment comes about in renouncement. That is the way in which we can escape from an existence replete with suffering. We shall now try to show in a few points how this basic law rules the whole structure of the human person, in such a way that it can be regarded quite simply as the essential presupposition of man's 'becoming man'.

Devotion as self-discovery

The very awakening to ourselves requires us to break through our 'being in ourselves' and to enter into otherness. We become conscious of the ego through a non-ego. We have to betake ourselves out of our subjectivity into the world of the object. Only and precisely when we 'go away' from ourselves, do we know that we are 'we'. Man is able to experience his inwardness only by taking something from outside into his inwardness. Already therefore, at this first, lowest plane of 'becoming man', the principle holds absolutely: 'He who wants to gain himself must lose himself.'

Knowing: self-renouncing openness of spirit

When we examine man's cognitive function, we find that knowledge is possible only when he ceases to insist on his own subjectivity. In order to know, man must—so to speak—'cut himself out', must listen to the truth of things that is independent of himself, must develop earthly 'piety'. Knowing must be governed by an unconditional quest for truth. The spirit must seek out reality itself in an attitude of devotion and self-renouncement. What is discovered, what is independent of the subject, is the final criterion of all knowledge.

Man must become very critical, indeed distrustful, in regard to himself. Man's cognitive attitude must not be dominated by any kind of 'approximation'. Truth can be encountered only by the utmost concentration on reality and the exclusion of subjective influences. Through the cognitive attitude, through objectivity that is really lived, man is detached from whims and self-will. Knowing involves an unsentimental, disciplined submission to facts. Sober clarity, an eye for essentials, objectivity without illusions, strict self-discipline, exclusion of all vagueness and 'easy solutions': these ought to be the determining factors of the mind.

It is only in such an attitude of renouncement that man finds his way to the holiness of being, to the purity and chastity of things. It is an unceasing measuring of the mind to the measure imposed by things. It demands a unique restraint, an apparently cool objectivity, a simple matter-of-factness, a spiritual humility which might almost be called innate, in fact a strict discipline of the whole man, to be acquired only in manifold sacrifices and renouncements. Man must rise to his task. He must attach more importance to what is outside himself, renounce egocentricism, lay himself open to the objective world. The greater this self-forgetting openness to the world, so much the more powerful becomes the vision of truth and so much mightier the knowing mind. Here, too, the principle holds in its whole extent: 'He who wants to gain himself must lose himself.'

Love: absorption in the 'thou'

The highest knowledge is realized in love. There is in reality a sphere of being which can be known only in love: the 'thou' of the other person, the personal depths, that inwardness where man in his uniqueness has his source. This deepest reality of the other person can be experienced solely as self-utterance. But the presupposition of every genuine self-utterance is that it is spoken into a sphere of personal trust, that is, of love.

Love creates a unity of being between two persons. This unity of being carries with it immediate knowledge of the other. Anyone who does not love a person has not known him in his truest reality. Love means being so dependent on another person that we ourselves receive our own being from him. I am myself by the fact of loving. But I love, because you are. I am, therefore, because and in so far as you are.

Anyone who knows man's inconstancy—indeed, his incapacity for loving—needs no long explanation as to what a venture is here involved. In love man surrenders himself into the hands of another person, whose nature, liberty, loyalty and existence are threatened, into whose life suffering can enter; and this—since the two lovers make up a unity of being—will then become his own suffering.

It is profoundly true that there cannot be any happy love in a world menaced by suffering. And yet there is no other way to happiness than by exposing ourselves to this menace. This is brought out clearly by C. S. Lewis:[8]

> To love at all is to be vulnerable. Love anything, and your heart will certainly be wrung and possibly broken. If you want to make sure of keeping it intact, you must give your heart to no one, not even to an animal. Wrap it carefully round with hobbies and little luxuries; avoid all entanglements; lock it up safe in the casket or coffin of your selfishness. But in that casket—safe, dark, motionless, airless—it will change. It will not be broken; it will become unbreakable, impenetrable, irredeemable. The alternative to tragedy, or at least to the risk of tragedy, is damnation. The only place outside Heaven where you can be perfectly safe from all the dangers and perturbations of love is Hell.

A person whom we love can poison our whole nature, make suffering our lot, destroy our career, disappoint our most cherished hopes. And yet love does not cease, if it is really love. All that must be clearly stated, if we are to discuss self-fulfilment in love without illusions and in a mature way. This much is indisputable: man gains his own nature only by loving; but this very love is a venture, an abandonment of self, a menace to his own life. If he does not accept all that, he closes up for himself the way

[8] *The Four Loves*, Bles, London, 1960, pp. 138-9.

to happiness. 'He who wants to gain himself must lose himself.'

Freedom from the ego, supreme form of self-possession

Freedom is really nothing other than the capacity to shape our final self-expression. Hence it strives for the final, unrepeatable and eternal: for the unconditional establishment of the conditioned, the final establishment of the provisional, the eternal establishment of the temporal, the irrevocable establishment of the revocable. It can indeed resist all this—that is why it is in fact freedom —but it does not thereby attain its fulfilment. This comes about only through the free affirmation of what must be affirmed, the free acceptance of what is demanded.

God gives us a heart so that we can freely give it back to him. Perfect freedom means to do the right—that which is known to be right—with the whole force of our nature, regardless of ourselves, not capriciously and not clinging to freedom, at each moment to be able to do all things and every thing. Man is more honoured and exalted by submitting to the eternal order of things, freely accepting it, than by giving way to the weaknesses and constraints of his own life. What ought to be and what can be is realized in those who accept in simple humility the destiny that God wills for them. In such men God grasps the world and leads it where he wills to lead it, that is, to fulfilment. Here too what Christ set up as the principle of real life has its full validity: 'He who wants to gain himself must lose himself.'

Human essentiality, grandeur bestowed

We all want to lead an 'essential' life, a genuine, full and significant existence: our existence ought to bear the

character of the unique and unmistakable; for as many
people as possible or—if there is no other way—then for
only one single person, we would like to be 'everything',
wholly indispensable, irreplaceable and accepted to the
ultimate depths of our being. We do not want to be average human beings. Every day we run up against the dark
wall of our mediocrity; we long for great experiences.
We would like to reach out beyond all that is accessible
and measurable. We long for a transformation of our
whole existence, which would make us quite unique,
utterly profound. We do not want to lead an 'un-
mysterious', dull life, 'known' and discussed by every-
body. Whether for happiness or suffering, we would like
to have a unique destiny. We would like finally to rid
our existence of this faint-heartedness, this lack of buoy-
ancy, this weariness and stupor, this meanness and fur-
tiveness, which dominate our whole life.

We cannot live without greatness. Existence falls apart
when the hope of human essentiality is taken away from
us. Our longing for it must be kept alive. Therefore man
must 'aim' beyond his actual state; he must be able to
advance towards an ever greater promise, otherwise life
dries up within him. Something attained always presents
to man the danger of constriction, unless there is a longing to take it on to greater things. This is the basic condition of man's boundless aspirations, as it can be seen in
the quite simple phenomena of daily life. Behind it all is
God. In our longing for grandeur there is worked out,
implicitly and unsystematically, the drama of man's quest
for God. But it is just here that our radical incapacity for
greatness is revealed.

True grandeur is a transcendent award. It is God's
gift. We do not receive it because we possess special gifts:

talents, discernment, originality, personal impact, our own mystery of life, depth of feeling. The way to radical greatness cannot be 'prescribed' for us. It lies where God, the perfecter, wills to come to us. But we encounter him solely when we commit ourselves to the humdrum, to becoming insignificant, to the sphere of simple brotherliness, to the will of God. Dietrich Bonhoeffer observes profoundly:

> What is God? Firstly, not a general faith in God, in God's omnipotence and so on. That is not a true experience of God, but merely a little prolongation of the world. Encounter with Jesus Christ! Experience of the fact that there is a reversal of all human existence in Jesus' 'being there for others' alone. Jesus' 'being there for others' is the experience of transcendence.... Our relation to God is a new life of 'being there for others'.... The transcendent is not infinite, unattainable tasks, but the attainable neighbour who happens to be present at any particular time.

When the visit of his mother and brethren was announced to our Lord, he pointed to the circle around him and said: 'Here are my mother and my brethren! Whoever does the will of God is my brother, and sister, and mother' (Mark 3.34–35). Brothers, for Jesus, are those who are united in the common acceptance of God's will. To be brother of Christ, in the deepest sense, is to enter into the will of the Father; and this again means entering into the humdrum, being ready to accept our mission precisely in this everyday life. God wants from us our ordinariness and nothing else. He wants us to return to littleness and precisely through that to surpass all that is great. He demands of us an unobtrusive approach, leaving others free, not imposing on them. Hence a man's reserve and humility are certain signs of the divine

grandeur growing within him. Greatness grows only out
of a freely accepted littleness of life, which loses itself in
the other. Out of this we might work out a whole theology of heaven, of eternal consummation, perhaps also a
theology of the Eucharist. But here it is sufficient to note
that our innate drive towards human essentiality can also
be fulfilled according to the same basic law: 'He who
wants to gain himself must lose himself.'

Finally a word has to be said about our most mysterious
and most fundamental vital impulse.

Becoming more one by renouncing oneness of being

Human existence in all its dimensions is dominated by
a longing to share in the being of others. This longing is
revealed predominantly in a drive towards awareness, to
knowledge, to love. In the last resort it is the allurement
which leads pantheists to maintain that our finite being
must one day be mingled with the divine essence. But it
is precisely this allurement which is the most serious
temptation of our created existence. What sort of bliss
would it be if we were no longer ourselves? In order to
be, we must face God eternally in an attitude of love.
Since love creates a unity of being, his life flows eternally
in us; we are therefore deified. But at the same time we
lose nothing of that bliss which a finite being feels when
it can say 'thou' to the Infinite. We become more one
by renouncing our drive for complete oneness of being.
Here also then, at the last outpost of the desirable and
attainable, we see the absolute validity of the principle
of human authenticity set up by Christ: 'He who wants
to gain himself must lose himself.'

Thus we have discovered the essential law of happiness, that is, the way in which we can escape suffering.

This law ('Deny yourself if you want to be happy') is not an unintelligible demand of God on our nature. By a careful examination of our most primitive human impulses we have brought out the goal of the primal dynamism of the whole world-reality, which seeks to reach its consummation through us. If we want to rid the world completely of suffering, we must freely consent to the annihilation of our existence. In our reflections on suffering and its mastery through self-detachment there is contained an important statement about human death: death is the peak of life. In death human existence is made completely void and can thus accept eternal consummation as a gift. But we shall reflect on this only in our next meditation. What we were able to say about human suffering, we have already said here. It is an evil: therefore God does not will us to live in it. His will is to liberate us from it. The sole way of liberation is whole-hearted selflessness, detachment from our suffering-laden life.

V

DEATH

In this fifth meditation we want to venture on a decisive step towards understanding the mystery of human suffering. At the very heart of the Christian message lies the shattering statement: the real origin of life is death. What happens to man in death is more wonderful than his creation. It is a new birth. But why is this so? Why does life rise out of death? This is the question to which we want to find an answer in our meditation. The answer runs: Because death offers us the first possibility of making a final decision, face to face with Christ, in complete freedom and with the utmost clarity of mind. Man in death becomes perfectly 'person' and therefore only in death can he make a perfect decision. In order to be able to grasp the full import of this assertion, we must first range a little more widely. We must first list the reasons which lead us to say that the real decision of man's life occurs at death.

DEATH AS FINAL DECISION

On the question of the 'Last Things' there has been a revolutionary transformation of perspectives in the most recent Catholic theology. Hans Urs von Balthasar rightly described eschatology as the 'storm-centre of theology'. The great change was brought about by raising the quite simple and at first sight insignificant and harmless question: what happens to the whole man at the moment of death? In trying to answer this question, theologians observed that they would have to think out afresh their whole doctrine of the 'Last Things' in the light of the answer they gave. The new answer, proposed almost simultaneously by different theologians, might be formulated in this way: in death there emerges the possibility of the first completely personal act of man; hence death is ontologically the favourable point for awareness, for freedom, encounter with God and decision for our eternal destiny.

This statement sounds perhaps a little too academic. What we want to suggest is this: only at the moment of death can man discard the strangeness of his existence; only in death does he become sufficiently master of his being to encounter Christ completely, with every fibre of his nature, and—in that confrontation—to be able finally to make his decision. According to this hypothesis, we would again have a possibility of decision: to be more precise, only in death would we have the first possibility of a complete, fully personal commitment. In this hypothesis, salvation is conceived as radically 'christological' and 'personal'. And nevertheless it renders intelligible the fact that salvation—brought by Christ and to be won through personal effort by each individual human being —is 'universal'. In death, confronted by Christ, every man has the opportunity of making his decision in full possession of his powers, in absolute clarity and in complete freedom.

Very much depends on a correct understanding of the expression, 'in death', so strongly emphasized in this hypothesis. It is not a question (firstly) of the state 'before

death'. We cannot really assume that someone posits his
first completely personal act in a state of agony of body
and soul, in the stupor of dying. But neither is it a question (secondly) of the state 'after death'. Our eternal
destiny is forever fixed after death. In death we have become 'final' to such an extent that afterwards nothing
can be altered in this finality. It is in fact a question here
of the 'moment of death itself'.

Moment of encounter with Christ

The protagonists of this theory conceive the moment
of death in the following way: when the soul leaves the
body, it awakens suddenly to its pure spirituality, is
wholly filled with light and brightness. It understands
instantaneously all that a created spirit can know and
understand; it sees its whole life concentrated into a
unity; it discovers therein Christ's call and leadership; it
stands also before the wholeness of the world and sees
how the risen Lord shines out there as the world's ultimate mystery. In death, therefore, man becomes free,
aware and capable of making a final decision; in this decision he accomplishes the clearest encounter of his life
with Christ; it is now impossible for him to pass Christ
by. He must decide, this way or that. What is decided
there—in death—remains for eternity, since man throws
his whole nature into this decision, becomes wholly decision. As so decided, he lives for ever. The whole of
man's eternity will be nothing but the ontological unfolding of what took place in that moment.

The arguments brought forward in support of this doctrine cannot be analysed individually here. But to indicate
the general line of thought, we may point to one consideration. These theologians appeal to a profoundly

human experience: man does not yet 'possess' himself. In his longing, he never ceases to live ahead of himself and is therefore nowhere able to pin himself down, to give himself a final shape; in order to be, he stumbles ahead into time; thereby he merely skirts—so to speak—his present moment, the 'point' at which he is really 'there'; he merely skirts his own life and does not really live it. He cannot unfold his nature, cannot live his life in all its richness wholly and undividedly.

Only in the moment when it is impossible to go further into the same, fragmented future, can he fully realize his nature. Here the streams of his life meet together. He 'is' finally: he no longer lives like a rushing mountain brook, but like a calm mountain lake, clear and deep, reflecting the whole world in its profusion. But this moment can occur only in the moment of death. For only in death can there simply be no more 'further' in the same direction, into the empty openness of time: in death a new life dawns for us, which is the unceasing, intensively lived present. Only in death, therefore, does man reach the total unity of his being; he gets away from the universal constriction and unease and enters into the depths of the world, into the 'heart of the universe'.

'New birth'

If we want to describe the event of death pictorially in the light of this hypothesis, then the ancient Christian symbol for death—the analogy of birth—suggests itself. At birth, the child is thrust violently—so to speak—out of the narrow space of the mother's womb; it must leave the protecting, familiar, secure shelter. It is abandoned to a complete 'breakdown'. Simultaneously there lies open a vast, new world, a new relation to the world, the world of light, colours, meanings, the world of being with others and of love. In death something similar happens to man: he is taken out violently from the narrow space of his previous worldliness; at the same time he enters into a new, essential relation to the world, extending into the vastness of the universe. In death therefore, on the one hand, man really 'goes under', in the sense that there is a 'nullifying', a violent withdrawal of his bodily worldliness; at the same time, he plunges down to the roots of the world and acquires a total presence to the world.

This ground of the world, to which man descends as he dies, is of its nature 'open to Christ', transparent therefore to the ground of all that is. Man in death is also confronted with what he always surmises in all his knowing, that towards which he unconsciously strives in all his willing, what he embraces in reality in all his loving. At this metaphysical centre he will make his final decision. Death, therefore, is birth. Man in his death enters a world wholly radiant with Christ. The cosmic Christ completely envelops it. In his whole being man stands before his Lord. He can no longer pass him by.

'Liberation to freedom'

Man must go through death in order to come in his wholeness close to God. During our earthly life we are still wandering at a distance from true reality. We are dominated by people, things and events, by our own longings and dreams. All this fills up space, within and without, draws man into its power. This multiplicity of things scarcely leaves space for God any longer in our thoughts. If he is to enter heaven, the possibility must be open to man—wholly independent and free, with his

whole human reality led back as it were to the essentials
of his being—of one day standing before God and deciding for him with his whole nature. But for this to take
place, everything must be taken away from him to which
he clings with every fibre of his reality. His things, his
possessions, his power, even his friends, people dear to
him, his hopes and dreams, all that he has built up and
achieved in his life. One day all masks must fall, all roles
too must come to an end: all the parts that man plays
before the world and before himself.

By experiencing death, therefore, man is liberated from
everything that prevented him hitherto from seeing God
face to face. Death therefore is liberation to true freedom.
Through death man is delivered up completely to his
God. He cannot any longer hide himself from God. His
soul is—so to speak—transplanted into that infinite field
where there is nothing but himself and his God. He
stands now face to face with the risen Lord. Christ himself had to make his own the death-struggle, dying and
death, so that every man who goes on the way of death
might meet him suddenly in blinding clarity, so that
every man—at least in death—would make a final decision, face to face with him.

Irrevocable decision

Here—in death—God has completely overtaken man.
By taking death on himself, he has closed up all ways of
escape. Man has to go through death. And in death he
will meet Christ irrecusably. Here the terrible adventure
into which man has thrown himself—the adventure of
keeping at a distance from God—comes to its end. Christ
is now standing there, before man in death: clearly seen,
luminously perceived, he calls man to himself with the

7

gesture of redeeming love. Christ will for ever stand
there, his love calling and seeking to give itself. If man
in death decides against Christ, it makes no difference to
Christ's love. But this love will burn him eternally, because he eternally experiences it as utterly close and
nevertheless rejects it (and this is hell). But if he decides
for Christ, then the same love of Christ becomes for him
eternal light and final perfection in infinite happiness,
the eternal acceptance of the closeness of our Lord
(heaven). Thus the decision in the moment of death is the
judgment itself.

DEATH AS THE 'PARTICULAR JUDGMENT'

By his Yes or No man finally passes judgment on himself.

It follows from this: No one is damned merely because
chance so brought it about, merely because—perhaps as
a result of an accident—he was suddenly called away into
eternity; because he had never properly known God
during his earthly life, because he was born into a family
where he never had any experience of love and therefore
also could not understand what is God's nature; because
he perhaps turned against a God in whom he saw merely
a legalistic God, a ferocious tyrant; because he was abandoned by men, misunderstood and inwardly wounded,
and thus turned in rebellion against everything, even
against God. Anyone who thinks otherwise does not
know what eternal self-damnation is.

It follows from this: No one attains eternal salvation
merely because he had pious parents; because his middle-
class prejudices prevented him from doing the evil he
would so much have liked to do; because he had the

chance, which milliards of men—perhaps better men
than he—do not have, of growing up in a part of the
world where, at least occasionally, something may still
be heard about Christ; because he happened to have a
pleasant manner and thus also knew what it means to
be loved and did not find it difficult to believe that God
also loved him. Anyone who thinks otherwise does not
know what eternal 'deifying' means.

It follows from this: God is not small-minded; he is a
truly great Lord. We are not damned unless we have decided against Christ, with our whole nature, in complete
clarity and with full reflection; but neither are we deified
unless we have embraced Christ in an intimate encounter,
with all the fibres of our soul. Where we were born,
where we died, what kind of character we inherited, all
this is completely irrelevant; every man has the possibility of deciding in blinding clarity, for or against
Christ. Man is not the toy of a 'small and mean' God.
Such a 'God' does not exist.

It follows from this: Every man has the possibility,
at least once, of meeting Christ, the Risen One, of knowing him personally; even the heathen, those milliards
who have not yet heard of Christ; even Christians who
have become heathens, to whom perhaps we have
preached a God who is boring and remote from reality,
a God whom they could never learn properly to love;
even those human beings who have simply remained
small children in matters of religion and morality,
although the rest of their capacities developed in a
thoroughly normal way and they were able to make their
way successfully in the complex structure of modern life;
even those human beings who hate God, because they
see in him—for example—an instrument of 'capitalist

exploitation' and have never known him in his true
nature; even the mentally defective and emotionally im-
mature, who were never able to understand anything
properly; even the unborn and children who died without baptism; finally, we ourselves who are too weak to
do what is good and whose hearts remain so cold and
empty. In the light of our proposed hypothesis, all have
the possibility of gaining their salvation in a completely
personal encounter with Christ.

It follows from this: We must all remain alert. What
and who gives us the assurance that we shall make the
right decision in death? The outcome of this decision
will depend on ourselves. There is no other standard by
which to judge the sincerity of our conversion except conversion itself at this moment. What we want to be in the
future, we must begin in the present. We must prepare
ourselves by the many small, individual decisions of our
life for the great, final decision in death. Life is 'practice
for the judgment'. We must convert ourselves—and, indeed, at once—if we sincerely want conversion in death.
Any postponement of this pre-decision is an existential
lie. We simply cannot go on living thoughtlessly and
leave everything over to the final decision. Who can guar-
antee that we shall again at the end overturn the whole
orientation of our lives? Only we ourselves. The idea of
a possible final decision in death is like all great Christian
ideas: it liberates and at the same time imposes demands.
The proposed hypothesis offers us the possibility of understanding the 'particular judgment', not as an item
added to the long list of so-called 'Last Things', but as a
dimension of the decision in death, as the final determina-
tion of our nature. It remains to be seen whether the same

argument will be successful also in the question of purgatory.

The hypothesis of the ultimate decision in death permits us to get rid of some incredible, unworthy and grotesque ideas of purgatory. The place of purification is certainly not a gigantic city of torment, a 'cosmic concentration camp', in which wailing, groaning and moaning creatures are punished by God. God's thoughts have a very different greatness. Purgatory could certainly be conceived as an instantaneous event, as the quality and intensity of the decision formed in death. In this case the encounter with Christ, the entry before his loving gaze, would be our final purgation.

Purgatory as encounter with Christ

With love and grace Christ looks on the person who is approaching him. But his gaze simultaneously penetrates to the innermost recesses, the most hidden places, and to what is most essential in human existence. To encounter God in the fiery gaze of Christ is indeed, on the one hand, the supreme fulfilment of our capacity to love; but, on the other hand, it is also the most terrible suffering of our nature. In this perspective, purgatory would be nothing but the passage through the fire of Christ's love, the event of the encounter with Christ in death. In this encounter, love for God breaks out of the depths of human existence and penetrates our whole nature. To do this, it must break down the layers and "deposits" of selfishness—what scholastic theology calls *reliquiae peccati*, 'the remains of sin'. Love for God does indeed still glow in the depth of that human soul which is in need of purification; but it is buried under the dust and ashes of man's egoism. The harder and more solid these deposits are, the more painful also will be the break-through to Christ. Man's whole existence must 'break out' with its last resources, open itself to the loving approach of Christ. According to this theory, then, in-dividual human beings in the moment of death would go through a process of purgation, varying in intensity with each person. Thus, instead of a difference in the time spent in purgatory, there would be a difference in the in-tensity of purgation.

Our sustaining intercession

At this point the objection may be raised: 'If purifica-tion in purgatory is an instantaneous event, why then should we pray for our dead? In any case, our prayer arrives too late.' Two different answers can be given to this objection. The one is philosophical, drawn from the concept of temporality. We shall leave this on óne side, so that our meditation—which, anyway, is not supposed to be an exercise in philosophical thinking—is not too much encumbered. The other answer, the more impor-tant and decisive, is theological.

For God all is present: for him our prayer and the death of the person for whom we are praying coincide; for him, the human being whom we love and whose decision we want to make easier by the support of our prayer is dying at the moment when we are praying for him. The situation is of course similar to that which holds in the widespread devotional exercise in honour of the Sacred Heart, the 'Holy Hour'. By their prayer and compassion, the faithful comfort their Saviour in the Garden of Gethsemane, in his human sorrow and dread.

And this consolation really 'consoles', since for God the two points of time exist simultaneously. Our intercession therefore can never arrive 'too late', since God by his very nature knows no before and after. Our aid to the deceased person always arrives at the right moment, even if we are praying for him decades after his death. His moment is always simultaneously our moment. His decision always occurs now, even if he long ago attained eternal bliss. At every moment of our time we can sustain him in the greatest decision of his life. Our theory of purgatory therefore in no way depreciates the devout intercession of the faithful, but gives a more profound, more human dimension.

DEATH AS A POSSIBILITY OF SELF-DAMNATION

Here we must reflect prayerfully—albeit very briefly—on one of the darkest mysteries of our existence, on the possibility of hell. We know from revelation that this possibility lies open to all of us. But the same revelation forbids us to assume of any concrete individual that he has in fact been abandoned to hell.

Inviolability of freedom

Christ repeatedly and emphatically forbade us to condemn any human being. To the sinful woman he said: 'Neither do I condemn you' (John 8.11). Man therefore is not an 'object of judgment', not even of the judgment of Christ. Only man can condemn himself. Damnation is never anything other than self-damnation. Christ is content simply to reveal his love. In face of this love, man must pass judgment on himself. Whoever utters in death the Yes of his life is not condemned. But whoever

says 'No' to Christ's love has already condemned himself. Any kind of judgment on Christ's side, therefore,
becomes superfluous. Judgment is nothing but the revelation of love and man's decision in face of this love.

If we try to penetrate further into this complex, we
notice that something final and definitive is stated here
about man. There is in man a sacred 'reserve', which even
Christ will not infringe. In this reserve—which is nothing
other than the radical freedom of the creature—a creature of God, even when it has fallen away from God,
may not be disturbed. Any kind of dishonouring of freedom would be an insult to God, the Creator of this freedom. Is this not the meaning of the mysterious statement
in the Epistle of Jude, 'when the archangel Michael, con-
tending with the devil, . . . did not presume to pronounce
a reviling judgment upon him' (9)? Peter's Second
Epistle even calls the fallen angels 'the glorious ones',
against whom 'angels before the Lord do not pronounce
a reviling judgment' (2.10–11). Freedom, any kind of
freedom, represents an absolute in the world. But the
absolute is simply untouchable, not to be manipulated.
Not even God can do anything if a creature—for instance,
man in death—tells him to his face: 'No.' In this consists
the glory, but also the awful menace of our freedom.

Damnation, self-chosen separation from God

With his 'No' uttered in the presence of Christ, clearly
known and revealed in love, man hurls himself into
eternal abandonment. In death man becomes wholly
'himself', completely overtakes himself and is thus able
—as he was not able during his earthly life—to express
his nature perfectly in an act of his whole being. If at
this moment of the clearest freedom he says his 'No',

then he says it with his whole nature, hardens himself completely in his denial; indeed, he himself becomes wholly and absolutely denial. He chooses himself for ever: he must therefore endure himself eternally, must grope around for all eternity, lost in the dark void of his own existence.

It is not as if Christ would close up against him the 'way out'. Christ receives his creature with love whenever and wherever the latter comes to him. Our Lord rejects no one. Hell is not simply a punishment for a past sin (now perhaps bitterly repented). It is sin absolutely speaking, an always present sin, accepted with the whole of a man's nature. It is the rejection of Christ's love, unceasing flight from God. If God were to cease to love the person who thus damns himself, hell too would instantly cease to be hell. But God cannot do otherwise than love. His nature consists in love. His love is perfectly independent of the way in which the creature responds to it. We cannot force God not to love. If at any moment, therefore, the damned person were to repent of his deed of self-damnation he would there and then be in heaven. But that is just what he will not do. And in that refusal his hell consists.

This self-chosen separation from God causes in the person who freely damns himself a profound conflict: an inward cleavage and a state of hostility to the world as a whole. These divisions serve to explain all the pains of hell, which are summed up by theologians under the concepts of *poena damni* (pain of loss) and *poena sensus* (pain of sense).

Separation from God: when we lose God, the eyes become blind to beauty, to life, to richness, to true reality.

Separation from oneself: the nature of the created spirit consists in the fact that it longs for God with its whole reality; separation from God therefore occasions in it a cleavage reaching down to its innermost being; the damned person hates what is most real in his own nature, that which makes him long for God.

Separation from the world as a whole: the world consists in God's love given bodily shape in the creature; creation everywhere bears the image of that which the damned person radically denies; man also is substantially planted into the world; he embodies the universe in himself. The damned person then lives in a world which he feels to be his enemy, which everywhere burns him, resists him; and this burning—since man bears the world within himself—penetrates to the most hidden fibres of human reality.

Imprisoned in the self in the midst of a world radiant with God

From all this it follows that hell is not a 'special place', but the same world in which the blessed also live in eternal happiness. God cannot in fact deliberately create an 'evil place'. By his very nature, he is incapable of doing that. If God creates anything, it is bound to be good, since God can allow something to come to be only by fashioning it according to his nature; if it were not made in his image, it would simply be a non-entity. But the damned are simply out of place in this world.

Imagine a day when the sky is blue, the sun embraces the world in its rising morning glow, the birds sing, man is utterly happy. What harmony, what joy! But take a fish out of the water to enjoy this wondrous beauty: for the fish it is hell. And that is how the damned person lives unhappily in a world utterly radiant with God. According to some biblical accounts (particularly in the Book of Job and in the Prophet Zechariah), the blessed and the damned live in the same place, in the same world, associate with one another and have the right to talk with God. In fact, it could not be otherwise. If it were, the damned would not suffer at all in their separation from God, from themselves and from the world; their state would certainly not be that which they established for eternity by their absolutely free 'No' in death.

We have thus tried to explain hell as the No of the decision in death turned into an eternal state, therefore as a dimension of death itself. The same holds—of course, with the tokens reversed—for heaven. In uttering 'Yes' with his whole being in death, man overcomes the terror of encountering God (purgatory), outstrips everything which in God is perilous to our finite nature. Man can now enter into the knowledge and into the love of Christ, which in fact is the very essence of heaven. It follows that heaven is nothing other than the decision for Christ turned into a state of being. Nevertheless, we would like to reserve to a special meditation—the last one—the description of our eternal life in heaven.

Instead of spending longer on the discussion of this hypothesis about death, we would like now to present an imagined experience of what may happen to us at death. We ought to try for once to imagine our own death. Reflecting on death in prayer, we ought not to try to imagine the death of others, but rather our own death. We have therefore composed this last part of our meditation in the first person. The individual pictures which occur in it are of course merely pictures and therefore are not to be understood as literally true.

DEATH AS A SOURCE OF LIFE

I am now lying there, on my death-bed, limp, weary and unable to move my limbs. I listen to the blood rushing in my veins, throbbing in my ears. Marvellous music of life which becomes more and more remote. Dimly I still see the world through purple veils, my eyes red with fever. Weariness vibrates in my whole nature and blots out the familiar faces of the world. Exhaustion becomes more and more dominant. I have no longer sufficient strength to break through the wall of my solitude.

Abandoned in human solitude

I have now become finally alone. Alone as never before in my life. The loved ones around me have to look on, inactive and powerless, while I am being driven into an inescapable whirlpool of solitude. Snatched away into un-relieved loneliness, departed to the furthest outposts of the world. That is what my dying means. I can no longer even cry for help. I am powerless, bewildered, helpless as a child confined in a dark place. I have been hurled into the great, gray mist of infinite distance, into unmov-ing, muted, silent helplessness. The things and people in my life suddenly cease to exist.

I plunge more and more deeply into the misty dark-ness. Where, in fact, am I being hurled? Out beyond all earthly shores. But the amazing thing is that I do not find it strange to be hurled out in this way. I am plunging into something I have always known. It is as if I already once experienced this—and, indeed, not only once, but often in my life. I am being carried away to where I have always been in my dreams, in my longings, to that region which I have always divined behind things, persons and events.

This perception now strikes me with singular clarity. All around me now is light. The dominion of darkness has now ceased. Everything that I ever wanted in my life is now here. Here there awaits me the first smile that I ever perceived on the face of someone I loved. Here there awaits me that greatness which I sought in love, fatherhood, motherhood and friendship. Here await me the rough affection of my father, the tender look of my mother. All this now becomes one, submerged in a wondrous light, a light that does not dazzle but heals. Everything is here. All that was beautiful and precious on earth I find here again. Everything merges into one, marvellously radiant; everything glows, beats like a single heart; everything surges and blazes up. I am at last at home and hold fast the universe.

I plunge into the sacrament of death, in which all individual sacraments are comprised. Everything here is cleansing water, crystal-clear, life-giving, and I am immersed into this fount of being. Everything here is the rustling wind of the Spirit, telling me of mysteries of which my heart never dreamed. Everything here is marvellous food, bread of life, blood of the Lord, fortifying and nourishing. Everything here is penitence and pardon. Everything here is spiritual power, commanding the world's adoration. Everything here is unction, peace, strengthening, satisfaction and homecoming. Here already, I was always at home. This was the one thing shining in the depths of all my dreams and desires.

Becoming one with the world in Christ

Behind this luminous creatureliness, into which I now plunge as I am dying, God himself now begins to shine out. My heart has now ceased to beat. But in the meantime I gained the heart of the universe. In my heart the whole world is concentrated. I am now standing face to face with the risen Lord, since everything around me and in me has become wholly transparent to him. This is the moment for which I have been secretly waiting during my whole life. I now utter the one word of which my love is still capable and which sums up my whole life, the dreams of mankind and the longing of the universe: 'Thou.' Out of that word there grows an eternal embrace. Out of the mighty destiny of death I make a personal decision of love. Out of abandonment to Christ I make a devotion which draws me into Christ himself.

This is God's moment. He thought of this moment already, milliards of years ago, when he created the world. He thought of it at every stage of the slowly ascending evolution of the world. He thought of it when he prepared his own coming, during the time he spent as a stranger, forsaken and unnoticed in a remote corner of our world. He thought of it during his terrible agony, in his death, when he broke through the wall of worldliness; in his descent, in what we call the descent into hell, when he entered into the heart of the world; in his resurrection and ascension, in which he filled the universe.

He went through all that and took it on himself, so that I might meet him, now in death, in the depths of the universe and of my own being, and utter the word full of love: 'Thou.' Saying 'thou' then snatches me out of my nothingness and creates new being in me. A new corporality arises in me, no longer imprisoned within myself but embracing the universe. Now I see everything again with bodily eyes: I see God and also all that I left behind me. Everything now is infinitely close to me and I embrace mysteriously all those who are around me, mourning; those too who are with God, awaiting me.

A new state of the world, which is called 'heaven', is opening out before me. Only now, after boldly and extravagantly making over my nature to Christ and thus gaining eternal happiness, do I realize with a new force how terrible, how annihilating was the other possibility on which I might have decided. If in death I had rebelled against this divine 'Thou', as Satan did, at the beginning out of sheer hatred thrusting God away from himself eternally, then I would have plunged into infinite solitude, into the choking gloom of confinement within myself, into self-damnation.

I become utterly calm and silent, losing myself in gratiture for the gift of the triune God: the eternally enduring gift of his love. An eternity which is an ever-new beginning, everlasting transfiguration, lies before me: a state of the world become one in love. Hence death is truly the peak of world-events, the source of eternal life. In it man plunges more steeply than can be conceived into unfathomable depths, but only in order to mount up again and surge over, like a rising breaker, into eternal consummation.

VI

ETERNAL LIFE

In this closing meditation let us turn our thoughts again to eternal consummation, to heaven. Christian life is essentially witness. It is not sufficient for a Christian to keep to the 'main points', to confess the truths of Christianity, to live according to Christ's moral requirements. He must let all this 'shine out' in his life. This light comes into Christian existence only when the Christian attempts by faith to experience heaven in his own life, to feel it as the true and essential reality and to live it out credibly for his fellow-men. Through the Christian's existence heaven must enter into the corporality of the moment, into the historicity of the destiny here and now being realized. The Christian ought to be a witness to the fact that life proceeds towards an eternal happiness. Therein lies the charismatic function of Christians in the world: to prove to the world that heaven exists. But to be able to do this, the Christian must first experience heaven for himself. This he does in contemplation, in prayerful effort to make the world of our experience reflect its eternal mystery. The way in which the Christian soul becomes aware of heaven is a mysterious process. This is what we shall discuss first.

EXPERIENCE OF HEAVEN

We learn of heaven, not as the conclusion of a process of abstract thinking, but as the centre of meaning of in-

numerable indications, connections; as the centre of our
fidelity, our longing, our love. The Christian must look
into his whole being and the whole world of his experience for the presence of heaven. This is the basic exercise of any sort of spiritual life. The individual pieces of
this experience may perhaps be quite insignificant, like
small glass fragments. But when we place them together,
they make up a wonderful mosaic of our eternal home-
land.

Experience of the closeness of God

At the centre of this rehearsal for heaven, the point at
which it really becomes meaningful, are the great experiences of grace in our existence. We ought often to recall
those hours when God was quite close to us, when we
directly experienced his nature. There are such hours in
the life of every one of us. They are a part of the priceless
secret of the Christian soul. They are therefore not to be
'discussed' here. On those occasions we divined something of the ultimate reality, knew that all the longings
of our heart will one day have their fulfilment.

Sense of the eternal

But then we ought also to recall those moments
in which the world became transparent in form. The
moments in which we perceived the one illuminating,
warming and glowing reality behind the innumerable
fluctuations of colours and lights in our world. Suddenly
out of the darkness of our existence there appeared something that is hidden in mystery, in a mystery into which
we can enter ever more deeply. We have known the
heights and, above these heights, something that transcends and overshadows everything; we have grasped in

the depths of the world something that leads to the most hidden, most inward and most abysmal reality.

Those were moments in which we felt the mystery of spring, something exulting in the far depths of spring's intoxication, something younger than all that is young, eternal spring, eternal youth; moments in which, as summer came upon us, we experienced overflowing fullness, eternal noon, things growing bright and clear, tides without ebb; moments in which we perceived through the autumn's beauty, on heights beyond our comprehension, that which survives all becoming and ceasing to be; moments in which we saw that winter conceals from us something more intimate than the innermost things of all. So we might continue. Everywhere, in every emotion, in every truly human experience, we shall discover a depth or a height that leads us out beyond our narrow world, into the dimensions of eternal consummation, into the immensities of heaven.

It is a shattering experience to see how an invisible beauty rises through the visible colours of the world. In the mystery of motherhood we divine eternal security; in that of fatherhood, unbroken power mightily transformed. Art opens up to us a world that is deeper, more alive and more real than the world of our daily activity. In love, we say to someone: 'You are eternal.' In all these experiences the world becomes transparent to something other than itself: to heaven.

Longing for the infinite

Finally, the Christian ought to make an effort to grasp the fact to which the Marxist Ernst Bloch drew attention in his work, *Prinzip Hoffnung* ('The Principle of Hope'): even in his most ordinary experiences, man is constantly going beyond himself. In imaginative fiction, in the drive for change, in the experience of nature, in music and in philosophizing, in painting and in poetry, in technics and in exploration, wherever man experiences human things, he dreams himself into a more beautiful, radically 'other' future. The desire for better things, for the more beautiful, never dies away. At the centre of all these dreams, at the point of convergence of all these longings, is heaven.

All we wanted to do here was to give some hints as to how the Christian can 'spread himself out' towards heaven: how through his superficial experiences he can experience something that transcends all experience, something that no eye has ever seen, no ear has heard, no human heart could ever grasp—heaven. But now we must try to penetrate more deeply into the mystery and learn therefore, not from the wise of the world, but from the simple.

Angels as symbols of heaven

If we were to ask a simple Christian about heaven, he would probably begin his answer by saying: 'Heaven is the place where angels are.' Heaven and angels are essentially connected in Christian imagery. Christ expressly stated that 'in the resurrection' we 'are like angels in heaven'. Hence the answer of the ordinary man, although incomplete, is profoundly true. When we reflect on the nature of the angels, we come a step nearer to that reality which is called heaven and where we shall all be like angels.

What is an angel? Romano Guardini, in his work *Der Engel in Dantes göttlicher Komödie* ('The Angel in Dante's "Divine Comedy" '), insists that the angels have largely become insipid beings in the feeling and imagination of modern times. After the end of the Middle Ages, the angelic figure experienced a 'sentimental degradation'. 'Anyone who wants to see what they really are and what is their place in Christian life, must forget most of what has emerged in the art of the last five or six centuries—to say nothing of devotional products—and learn first of all from the Old Testament.'

Perfect self-realization in sharing God's life

In biblical revelation the angel is not the touching, kind-hearted escort who protects the child from falling from a bridge or from being bitten by a snake. The angel is God's earliest creation. God alone is the whole content of his life. His existence consists in sharing the divine life by love, vision, praise and service. His vitality arises from the fact that he has decided for God with his whole being. This decision took place at the first moment of his existence. For he is pure spirit and therefore perfectly simple. In every one of his deeds his whole being is concentrated. His first moment was already awareness in the utmost clarity, alert freedom, absolute self-realization: a gigantic deed at the very beginning of life, similar to man's decision at the moment of death.

If we try for once to gather together the totality of our spiritual experiences—experiences of grandeur, of ecstasy, peace, longing, purity, boldness and above all love—then we grasp something that we might regard as the shadow of the angel. Rilke understood something of the nature of the angels when he called them

> Early successes, favourites of fond Creation,
> ranges, summits, dawn-red ridges
> of all forthbringing,—pollen of blossoming godhead,

junctures of light, corridors, stairways, thrones, chambers of essence, shields of felicity, tumults of stormily-rapturous feeling.[1]

Manifestations of the God of power

We find, for example, in the Old Testament the account of Jacob's struggle. A man attacks Jacob as he is waiting, alone in the night. He is terrifying, strong, commanding, veiled in mystery. He is a creature, therefore a finite being, the angel of God. And yet he is also God's messenger in the tremendous sense that in some way he brings the sender, that is, God himself. When an angel appears in the Old Testament there occurs something sacred, glorious, but also at the same time terrible and horrifying.

In the New Testament this terror, this fierceness of the angelic nature is mitigated. But even here something terrifying clings to them. When the archangel appears at the side of the altar of incense or comes to Mary, when an angel stands before the shepherds in the field and the glory of God shines around him, when on Easter morning with blazing countenance he opens the grave and appears to the women, his first word is always: 'Do not fear!'

Again, in John's 'Revelation', the angelic figures rise to overwhelming heights. They are world-beings, cosmic

---

[1] *Frühe Geglückte, ihr Verwöhnten der Schöpfung,*
Höhenzüge, morgenrötliche Grate
aller Erschaffung,—Pollen der blühenden Gottheit,
Gelenke des Lichtes, Gänge, Treppen, Throne,
Räume aus Wesen, Schilde aus Wonne, Tumulte
stürmisch entzückten Gefühls.

—Rilke, 'The Second Duino Elegy'. Translation by J. B. Leishman, *Rainer Maria Rilke, Selected Works*, II (London, Hogarth Press, 1960).

essences. A mighty angel comes before the sealed book and in a voice of thunder announces the world's fate. Four others stand at the ends of the earth and bind the winds. Seven stand before God with golden trumpets, the blast of which brings endless terror to the world. One comes before the altar with a golden censer, fills it with fire and flings it down to earth. Finally, there is that angel of power who comes down from heaven, wrapped in a cloud, the rainbow above his head, his face like the sun, his legs like pillars of fire, who places his right foot on the sea and his left on the land, calling with a loud voice like the roaring of a lion.

Constantly present

According to revelation, therefore, angels are not tiny, pretty, touching and dainty beings. They so far transcend everything human that, if they enter our sphere, the might of their being is a threat to our very existence. They are the light and warmth of creation, beings wholly caught up in vision, adorers in deepest concentration, explorers of the depths of the Godhead. For them the limits of space and time do not exist. They ascend, penetrate, traverse the whole cosmos. In the scale of being, the angel is essentially the one who penetrates everywhere; hence, in our imagination, one who flies. Hence also the symbol of wings. The angels stand before God. But that means: they are present everywhere. In St Paul's theology they are 'principles of the world' (cf. Gal. 4.3; Col. 2.8), out of which as it were things proceed, to turn their visible shape towards us. Behind things, facts and historical events are angels, attending us everywhere, unceasingly, present by the very fact of their being. That is why our world is holy and the inner space of creation already heaven.

Occasionally and in selected passages the presence of angels takes on an immediately tangible shape. So, for example, in children and in helpless people. Behind the weak—but predominantly behind children, who are indeed given over to us wholly without defence—according to our Lord's words, is God himself in the form of the angel. If we do harm to them, we encroach upon something that leads directly to the hidden things of God. Here, incidentally, the sacred dignity of the helpless person becomes clear. The child is a point at which the presence of angels becomes tangible in this world. The child, because it is helpless. The same thing occurs to whatever is helpless. The angel is present especially where helplessness arises from the innermost nature of the creature, where being becomes tender and holy, where life tends inwardly. There, everywhere, are angels. There, heaven is opened.

This cursory meditation on the nature of angels—albeit merely in a first approach—has brought us closer to answering the question about the nature of heaven. For in heaven we shall all become like angels. At present we must leave aside the question as to how we shall then be like these terrible, glorious creations of God. The answer to it will become clear of itself by the end of our meditation. The point of these introductory reflections was to show that we must think grandly of heaven—for the presence of which the angels are only a feeble sign—and dismiss all mean and prettifying ideas.

We may be permitted now to raise another preliminary question, concerned with something apparently of secondary importance, but which will lead us close to the essential definition of heaven. The question is: Where is heaven?

In the history of religion, two fundamentally different answers have been given to this question.

The one basic form of religiosity, the so-called 'uranian' or 'sky' religions, the influence of which has been very strong on us Christians, looks for the place of God—heaven—'above'. This religious attitude sprang from the hunters' and nomadic shepherds' sense of the world, that is, from the feeling of men who experienced the mystery of the starry skies and the sun's warmth with all the fibres of their existence. But in the course of time it acquired another interpretation. The 'above', where God dwells, is not an 'above' in space, but in meaning. It is that sphere of being which absolutely transcends all mundane reality, the place of withdrawal, that which we can touch only with an absolute effort of our whole nature, by climbing above and beyond all things. God dwells in absolute transcendence. He is the one who 'lies utterly far out, wholly beyond' everything, the humanly unattainable.

This absolute 'above', for us Christians, is Jesus Christ, the risen Lord. In his ascension he broke through the walls of the world, climbed up, not to the stars, not into world-space, but absolutely 'high'. And this height he filled with his divine-human reality. 'Above' is where the risen Lord is. Every stirring of the heart, aimed at an 'above', every effort to reach 'upwards', is a movement to our Lord.

The other basic form of religiosity, the so-called 'chthonian' or earth religions, looks for the place of God

—heaven—'below', or rather 'within', in the 'depths'. This basic religious attitude sprang from the planters' and agricultural people's sense of the world: the feeling, therefore, of men who experienced in a religious way the earth's fertility and who had to struggle unceasingly with the untamed power of tropical vegetation.

This inwardness, this seclusion, again must not be conceived 'spatially'. It is depth in meaning. It does not lie, for example, at the centre of the earth or at another spatially definable point. It is the sphere which lies wholly below, on the other side of reality, 'beyond it all inwardly', deeper than our heart, deeper than the soul's roots, deeper than all the world's depths. By this is meant the pure immanence of God. In the innermost depths of all inwardness also God dwells and in the form of a withdrawal into the universe. Into this sphere of the pure inwardness of the world and the soul Christ went, in his descent, in what we call the descent into hell: into the heart of the earth. He thus became the absolutely inward and secluded reality of the cosmos.

Entry into the presence of God

Christ then for us is still inaccessible and secluded, absolutely high and deep. This inaccessibility and seclusion of Christ will cease in heaven: that is, by the removal of this inaccessibility and concealment, heaven will be created. Therein every being will shine out. God will be 'there' finally, in pure presentiality. That is heaven.

All inwardness has found expression, all concealment has become evident. Outwardness is full of depth. Everything is fulfilled, everything is one. There is no longer anything inaccessible, no longer anything concealed.

9

What was inaccessible and concealed is now openly available.

God—that is, God in Christ—is now no longer 'outside' and 'inside' the world: he has himself become the world, the very life of our living space. Or, as the New Testament expresses it, he is now 'all in all'. A tremendous assertion. Through all that belongs to the world there shines Christ's fullness of light, the infinitely abundant fullness of blessing and beauty. This Christ, who is 'all in all', will therefore be our location in heaven. Heaven therefore is not another place, not another world, but a new state of the world, precisely that state in which Christ is 'all in all'. Everything will be elevated into his divine-human existence and filled by him to the very brim. The whole creation, the whole wealth of our world-structure—sun, moon, stars, spaces, earth, sea, islands, mountains, plants, animals—everything in heaven is the dimension of Jesus Christ, the risen Lord.

Self-revelation of Christ

Christ already accomplished this transformation of the universe in his fourfold-single deed of redemption and consummation: that is, in his death and descent, in his resurrection and ascension. In the eucharistic food also he became the vital principle of our existence. But this union of the Christian and the world with Christ is not yet evident. It still lies in a sacred reserve, in the sphere of the inaccessible and concealed. In heaven, where all that is inaccessible and concealed will be open—that is, what is above climbs down and what is below reaches the heights—everything that we already bear within us, everything that we now possess, becomes the essential sphere of life. Becoming open is therefore the central factor of heaven's coming to be. Christ's self-revelation founds heaven.

Heaven occurs for us when—as Paul says in the Epistle to the Ephesians—'we attain to unity in the knowledge of the Son of God, ... to the measure of the stature of the fullness of Christ' (Eph. 4.13), when therefore we know Christ openly in the fullness of his being, in his dimensions encompassing mankind and the whole universe. That, incidentally, is the 'definition' which our Lord himself gave of heaven: 'this is eternal life, that they may know him whom thou hast seen' (cf. John 17.3). Heaven therefore means first and foremost: knowing Christ.

'KNOWING CHRIST'

'Knowing' in biblical usage does not mean a purely intellectual process, but 'two beings becoming one in love'. We read in Genesis: 'Adam knew Eve his wife and she conceived and bore Cain' (Genesis 4.1). Two human beings becoming one in the love of body and soul offers only a feeble likeness of that supreme knowing which takes place between the redeemed person and Christ: inward participation in his personal reality, loving union with him, in which his whole nature shines out before us and becomes ours. Therein everything that he bears within himself becomes ours: the whole cosmos, all mankind, all the richness and beauty of the earth, and—at the deepest level—the Holy Trinity. Already now we bear all that within us. But not yet as a state of existence laid open. In heaven it will all be—so to speak—part of our nature, lived, felt, experienced, real and inseparable. What we have said is expressed by John in his first Epistle in this way: 'Beloved, it does not yet appear what we shall be; but we know that when Christ appears we shall be like him, for we shall see him as he is' (3.2).

Unceasing renewal in absolute fulfilment

'Seeing' in this text is another word for that 'knowing' of which we were hitherto speaking. It is the expression for supreme union with God, for man's ec-static being beyond himself in God and for God's in-static being in us. 'Seeing' as understood here transforms our whole being into a capacity for projecting into the Godhead. It is a loving gaze of God towards us and our loving gaze towards God. A process in which all creation becomes clear as crystal.

This, however, implies in no way—as it is often (falsely) imagined and represented—an immobile, rigid, wooden staring at an external drama, but an eternal bringing forth—indeed, a creation—of the world out of our vision. Rest—a concept often used with reference to eternal bliss—certainly does not in any way mean torpidity. Nothing in heaven is stiff and motionless. On the contrary, everything is at full strain in concentrated activity. Eternal rest is the mode of this persistent being in motion: tranquillity, composure, leisure, effortlessness of being and possessing.

The impossibility of conceiving heaven as rigidity arises from God's infinity, from the inexhaustibility of his being. If God is in the most radical sense infinite, then our being-with-God in heaven must be conceived as an unceasing growing into, proceeding into God. Being-with-God is then simultaneously a never-ending ascent to him. Standing and moving at once. Because there is no limit to God's being, our eternal community of nature with him must necessarily be without limit, ever more receptive.

This dialectic of eternal bliss could come to an end only if our nature were wholly to coincide with God. But, since this can never be, on account of God's infinity and inexhaustibility, it continues into eternity. Unceasing renewal in absolute fulfilment: that is the structure of our eternal bliss. It is the state in which satiety and weariness are not to be expected, in which desire is not relaxed by fulfilment and longing still maintains its ardour in delight. Our yearning, absolutely fulfilled, will engender in heaven a fresh longing for God. And that for the whole duration of endless eternity.

Abundance of life

St Thérèse of Lisieux, living wholly on her sense of the closeness of heaven, given to her by faith, gained her first, unforgettable impression of heaven when reading these words of the Abbé Arminjon:

> God speaks with gratitude: Now it is my turn! What other answer can I make to the gift in which my elect have offered themselves than to give myself utterly. If I laid in their hands the sceptre of creation, if I clothed them with streams of light, that would be a great deal—more than they would have ventured to desire and hope. But it would not be all my heart longs to give. I owe them my life, my nature, my eternal and infinite being. I must be the soul of their soul, penetrate them and saturate them with my divinity, as fire saturates iron. By showing myself to them, unconcealed, unveiled, I must unite myself with them in an eternal face-to-face encounter, so that my glory may illumine them, penetrate them and stream out of all the pores of their existence, that they may know me as I know them and thus themselves become gods.

Christ promises to each his own happiness in heaven: that for which he longs more than anything else. To the Samaritan woman eternal water. To the people of Capernaum bread of eternal life. To the fishermen overflowing nets. To the Judean shepherds great flocks and ever-green pastures. To the merchants infinitely precious pearls. And to all of us again and again an eternal banquet, a continual wedding feast: symbol of infinite happiness in belonging to the dearest person in our life. To the Greeks the apostles then promise what means to them the greatest happiness: knowledge, understanding, infinite assurance in a harmonious spiritual city, solemn processions, translucent being which is made up of shining precious stones. And all that, as the Book of Revelation continually assures us in constantly varying images and scenes, will be offered in enduring freshness and never-ending variety. But all these gifts of happiness and repletion are not there for their own sake, but flow towards us as surging waves of Christ's self-giving.

God 'all in all'

What occurs here is beyond our imagination, but we must believe it, for our Lord himself said: 'Blessed are those servants whom the master finds awake when he comes; truly, I say to you, he will gird himself and have them sit at table, and he will come and serve them' (Luke 12.37). God himself, this God for ever serving us, will become for us 'all in all'. Not that things, persons and events cease to be themselves, but that God himself approaches us in them, in a thousand forms, and by his mighty presence elevates their small, finite reality and turns them into infinite gifts.

The vision of what we now divine of things concealed,

the perception of what is occasionally heard as out of an eternal silence through the uproar of the world, the tentative reception of what we touch now already in its earthly forms, but can never really hold: that will be heaven. Not the neoplatonic world of ideas—glorious, but bloodless and emaciated—but the fullness, the fine figure elevated to infinity of our sensible perceptions which directly encase God as gift.

There will take place that ineffable event for which the Church prays in the hymn to the Holy Spirit: *accende lumen sensibus.* God's light will flash out in all our senses. What the mystics and also deeply religious people now already experience in innumerable reflections will come to pass: God is seen, heard, touched and tasted by us. Thus in heaven everything spiritual is transposed into the realm of sense and everything sensible into the realm of spirit. Even God. And man becomes wholly aware of all reality, which is body and spirit, shape and light, being and meaning in one—the world in its wholeness. All pantheism is merely childish fantasy when compared with this ultimate union of God with creation, in which diversity is not abolished, but the intensity of the blending continually increases.

Entire self-becoming

This immediacy to God makes it possible for us to become wholly ourselves. Already here in our earthly life—particularly in love—we learn that we become really 'we ourselves' only by getting away from ourselves, freeing ourselves from ourselves. In heaven the whole person now becomes self-giving, the very dissolution of self, 'self-forgetfulness into God'. The greedy hold man has hitherto kept on himself is now released and our whole

being lies there, a radiant gift held out by the loving hand
of self-giving. In heaven we become utterly small and
precisely in this way we become great, reach absolute per-
manence of being. It is a drowning and being lost in the
infinite richness of God's life, but it does not mean that
we cease to be creatures. Man loses himself and his being
lost makes him perfect.

Something similar occurs in the Eucharist: the created
thing becomes so small, abandons itself so radically, as
to lose its proper reality, its substance, to Christ. We lose
ourselves completely in God and receive ourselves back
in our wholeness and deified. Thus man in heaven becomes 'himself'. All that we strove for in life, half-
realized, and also all that we could not be, what existed
for us as concealed, denied, still-born possibility now
blooms into full reality. And we know that we never lost
anything, least of all what we renounced in life.

Corporality penetrated by spirit

Our body itself becomes our person, the perfected expression of our inner being. A body which we create for
ourselves in the power of God and not—as in our earthly
life, with all its constraints and predeterminations—
merely received from our parents. A body shaped by the
new and never-ending might of the Spirit, wholly
coming forth from the divine and constantly plunging
back into the divine. That body alone is wholly perfected
which is completely assumed into the spirit. What man's
body really means becomes clear only in heaven, in the
state of resurrection and transfiguration. Not set up for
itself, not a barrier against the world, against men and
against God, but the expression of a whole and entire
union with the universe.

In an absolute abandonment to Christ, therefore, we become in heaven 'we ourselves'. That is the basic law of spiritual creation: for each one the best fruits are plucked by a hand that is not his own. Hence it incidentally becomes clear also that we shall find heaven not so much in ourselves as in the other persons—above all, in Christ, but also in other risen and transfigured human beings—and only subsequently—in the midst of the love flowing back from the others to us—in ourselves. That is the next basic characteristic of heaven. It is the state, now fully realized, of being together in love.

BEING TOGETHER IN LOVE

The people we loved during our life become heaven for us. The beloved 'thou' in heaven turns into eternal happiness. Our love for one another, transfigured, creates a new sphere of existence. Lovers incidentally experience now, already in earthly life—admittedly only obscurely and mysteriously—a similar transfiguration of the world in the light of love. Everywhere, even now, love exercises its magic. The street, the town, where the beloved lives, seems made of gold, becomes a festive scene. That name blazes out on stones, bricks and lattices. In heaven all this becomes reality, reality still creating being.

The bright glances of those who love in heaven, lost in one another, make up the new, radiant cosmos. In their eternal being-together, in their ever-enduring embrace, new being arises. We experience the warmth, the radiance, the vitality, the overflowing richness of the person we love: we rejoice with him and thank God for him. His whole being, the fullness of his soul, the spaciousness of his heart, the creativity, comprehensive-

ness and inspiration of the love on his side finally becomes
a gift to us.

Through the past joys of his earthly life he has become
still more capable of joy, more receptive to joy, and in
our being-together we shall relive every happy hour we
spent with one another. And what he experienced as hard
and bitter now remains in eternity as potent victory, as a
triumphal arch of indestructible life. All past struggles
live on in him as a great capacity for love. The blows of
fate have left behind a marvellous tenderness and gentle-
ness in his nature in which now all things, all persons,
the whole world, can make their mark and find expression. Everything dark that he has ever looked on has
made his eyes bright and more alert for eternal vision.
His eyes: they now shine with innocence like the eyes of
a child and yet remain sharp and penetrating. There is
now a mildness, a harmony and a repose in these eyes
and all things are at home in their gaze.

His whole being is a centre of repose and balance of
harmony and rhythm. He has become the ruler of the
world, regal, secure, alert and courageous. His wisdom
is a single vision reaching into the depths of God, en-
veloping all things with an abysmal and yet all-embracing
gaze. Thus that person in heaven will be every person—
indeed, in some way, all mankind in each of its repre-
sentatives—whom we love; and in their love, now turned
into a state of being, we shall find our eternal home. Their
love and their being become for us the everlasting centre
of being.

THE SECOND COMING OF CHRIST

One of the most profound conceptions of Christian theology is that Christ has indeed come, but is continually

coming until the end of the world. The birth of Christ takes place throughout the whole course of history. To the end of time Christ still comes to be. Christians build up his body. From this standpoint we can see what constitutes the essence of Christian life. By the fact of being Christians we transpose ourselves into Christ, grow together with him, become Christians.

Paul sees the true mystery of being a Christian in the fact that Christ exists in the believer and the believer in Christ. We are absorbed into Christ's existence but without thereby losing our own personality. This process of becoming one with Christ is called "Christian life" and death is its fulfilment. Therefore, when once the measure of Christ is full, when all who are to make up his fullness —his *pleroma*—have died to him, then the 'cosmic Christ' is born, then he will appear. And with him we too shall appear. Our life hidden in Christ becomes open, turns into a state of being. That is the meaning of the mysterious event described in the Epistle to the Colossians: 'Your life is hid with Christ in God. When Christ who is our life appears, then you also will appear with him in glory' (3.3–4). Under the veil of things, therefore, a sacred cosmos slowly arises.

One day, when Christ has attained his 'cosmic fullness of age', the tension between God and the world will be relieved. Like lightning going from one pole to the other, Christ will suddenly reveal himself. His presence will break through all barriers and flood the universe. The universal Christ, the sun of eternal promise, will rise on the universe. At that moment, Christ—who gathered mankind into himself and through it the whole universe —will give himself up to the Father's embrace. The dream of all mysticism will have found its perfect

fulfilment: God will be all in all, *Erit in omnibus omnia
Deus*. At the end is a world wholly transformed into
God's transparency.

A man of deep prayer, who knew from inner experience the spiritual, mystical structure of the world, once
described our entry into heaven in these words. 'The
beginning'.

'The Beginning'

'Suddenly roused out of the agony of dying, become
wholly myself, in a decision for God drawing on all the
reserves of my existence, a new world, spiritually transparent, is laid open before me. Troops of glorified beings
stream towards me. All heaven circles around me as
around its truest centre. Admiration and love rise up towards me, even the angels' adoration. Adoration: not
directed to my weak, created, petty and negligible being,
but to him whose transparent vessel I have become.
Everything around me lies there as in the purest noon-
day light of divine love. With what has now become a
regal bearing, I pass through the worshipping figures in
whom all reality is concentrated until suddenly I am
seized by a feeling of holy terror, familiar indeed, but
only now experienced in its fullness and rushing through
all my veins: God is here.

'Now I stand dumb, since it is not for me to speak.
The divine persons now come towards me. They thank
me for believing in their love. They admire me: the puny
being that a thoughtless touch could reduce to nothing
and whose best thoughts hitherto contained things which
—if they had thought them—would in a flash rob the
angels of their light. They admire me for gaining heaven.

Suddenly I know that I am nothing, although I have achieved things so great that the heights of heaven are moved to wonder at them.

'All is gift. The divine persons now tell me how restless their heart was until it found rest in me. They bestow everything on me. Their knowledge, so that I may know the universe and all men—and the angelic hearts. Their will, that I may sanctify all being for loving service. Their love, that I may be able to encompass them with their own love and in them all that is. My voice is stilled.'

And the voice must be stilled, in order to leave the heart alone with its prayerful conjectures. It must not fear to depict heaven in its own imagery. Human images are holy and we have a right to humanize the divine and the heavenly. Nothing that we can do for all eternity can compare with the irrevocable humanization of God which took place at the Incarnation.

So we come to the end of our meditations on sickness, suffering and death. All ended in divine joy. This calm, unobtrusive joy the Christian ought to carry out into a world which knows so little joy and so much suffering. He must not be horrified by the emptiness of his own heart. Our Lord promised that streams of living water would flow out from us. If we try—not hastily, not selfishly and stubbornly, but simply and calmly trusting in God—to be ready for the unmeritable gift of God, in the midst of the world, in the midst of our calling, then even unconsciously and without our intending it streams of living water of divine joy will break out from us.